Cambridge Direct Mathematics

Reception: Summer

Teacher's Handbook

AUTHOR Elizabeth Toohig

CAMBRIDGE
UNIVERSITY PRESS

PUBLISHED BY THE PRESS SYNDICATE OF THE UNIVERSITY OF CAMBRIDGE
The Pitt Building, Trumpington Street, Cambridge, United Kingdom

CAMBRIDGE UNIVERSITY PRESS
The Edinburgh Building, Cambridge CB2 2RU, UK
40 West 20th Street, New York, NY 10011-4211, USA
477 Williamstown Road, Port Melbourne, VIC 3207, Australia
Ruiz de Alarcón 13, 28014 Madrid, Spain
Dock House, The Waterfront, Cape Town 8001, South Africa

http://www.cambridge.org

First published 2002

Printed in the United Kingdom at the University Press, Cambridge

Typefaces Frutiger, Swift   *System* QuarkXPress® 4.03

A catalogue record for this book is available from the British Library

ISBN 0 521 01128 0 paperback

Author Elizabeth Toohig

Contributors to CMD Summer Teacher's Handbook: Caroline Buck,
Pete Crawford, Julia Evans, Paul Jackson, Katie Tilley, Elaine Voice

Cover illustration by Lizzie Finlay

Text illustration by Tim Oliver, except page 18 (Anne Dalton),
page 24 (Beccy Blake) and page 26 (Bethan Matthews)

Project management by Cambridge Publishing Management

The author and publishers would like to thank the many schools and
individuals who trialled lessons for Cambridge Mathematics Direct.

The author and publishers would like to thank Sue Atkinson, Sharon
Harrison and Laurie Rousham for permission to use ideas from *First Skills in
Numeracy 1* © 1998 Cambridge University Press

Abbreviations and symbols

IP   Interactive Picture
IP
4

AS   Activity Sheet
AS
5

Italic text has been used for questions for the teacher to ask.

SP indicates Solving problems objectives

Topics:

CR = Counting, reading and writing numbers

CO = Comparing and ordering numbers

AS = Adding and subtracting

M = Comparing and ordering measures

SS = Exploring pattern, shape and space

Contents

Introduction

Ideas banks and lesson plans

> **Key idea** Numbers can be written as words.

> **Key idea** We say the next number name when we count forwards.

> **Key idea** Counting back from 67 to 62 is like counting back from 7 to 2.

> **Key idea** We can use numbers to make games.

> **Key idea** We can use different ways to help us count.

Matching to the NNS Framework objectives

This grid matches Cambridge Mathematics Direct lesson objectives to the teaching programme from the National Numeracy Strategy *Framework for teaching mathematics,* to help you in your planning. These objectives incorporate those of the *Early learning goals.* See page 12 for more planning ideas.

Framework objectives	Lessons
Counting and recognising numbers	
Counting	
● Say and use the number names in order in familiar contexts such as number rhymes, songs, stories, counting games and activities (first to 5, then 10, then 20 and beyond)	CR10.1
Recite the number names in order, continuing the count forwards or backwards from a given number	
● forwards	CR10.2, 10.4, 11.1, 11.2
● backwards	CR10.3
Count reliably up to 10 everyday objects (first to 5, then 10, then beyond), giving just one number name to each object	CR10.5
Begin to recognise 'none' and 'zero' in stories, rhymes and when counting	CR10.1
Count reliably in other contexts, such as clapping sounds or hopping movements	CR10.2
Count in 10s	CR12.1–12.3
Count in 2s	CR13.1–13.5
Estimate a number in the range that can be counted reliably, then check by counting	CR11.1–11.5
Reading and writing numbers	
Recognise numerals 1 to 9, then 0 and 10, then beyond 10	CR10.2
Begin to record numbers, initially by making marks, progressing to simple tallying and writing numerals	CR10.4
Comparing and ordering numbers	
Use language such as more or less, greater or smaller, to compare numbers and say which is more or less, and say a number which lies between two given numbers	CO3.1, 3.2
Order a given set of numbers: for example, the set of numbers 1 to 6 given in random order	CO3.1
Order a given set of selected numbers: for example, the set 2, 5, 1, 8, 4	CO3.2
Begin to understand and use ordinal numbers in different contexts	CO3.3–3.5

Adding and subtracting

In practical activities and discussion:	
Begin to use the vocabulary involved in adding and subtracting	AS5, AS6
Begin to relate addition to counting on	AS5.1, 5.4
Begin to relate the addition of doubles to counting on	AS5.2
Find a total by counting on when one group of objects is hidden	AS6.1
Begin to relate subtraction to 'taking away' and counting how many are left	AS6.2
Remove a smaller number from a larger and find how many are left by counting back from the larger number	AS5.3, 5.4, 6.2
Begin to find out how many have been removed from a larger group of objects by counting up from a number	AS6.3
Work out by counting how many more are needed to make a larger number	AS6.3, 6.4

Reasoning about numbers or shapes

Talk about, recognise and recreate simple patterns: for example, simple repeating or symmetrical patterns from different cultures	CR12.1, 12.2, 12.3, 13.1, 13.3, 13.5 SS5.5, 6.1
Solve simple problems or puzzles in a practical context, and respond to 'What could we try next?'	M3.5
Make simple estimates and predictions: for example, of the number of cubes that will fit in a box or strides across the room	CR11.1, 11.2, 11.3, 11.4, 11.5 M3.1, 3.2, 3.3, SS6.1
Sort and match objects, pictures or children themselves, justifying the decisions made	SS5.1, 5.3

Problems involving 'real life' or money

Using developing mathematical ideas and methods to solve practical problems involving counting and comparing in a real or role play context	AS5.2, 5.3
Begin to understand and using the vocabulary related to money • sort coins, including the £1 and £2 coins, and use them in role play to pay and give change	AS5.3, 5.4, 5.5, 6.5

Comparing and ordering measures

Use language such as more or less, longer or shorter, heavier or lighter ...
to compare 2 quantities, then more than 2, by making direct comparisons
of lengths or masses, and by filling and emptying containers

- length   M3.1
- mass   M3.2
- capacity   M3.3

Begin to understand and use the vocabulary of time
- begin to read o'clock time   M3.4
- begin to be aware of the duration of time   M3.5

Exploring pattern, shape and space

Use language such as circle or bigger to describe the shape and size of
solids and flat shapes
- begin to name solids such as cube, cone, sphere, ...   SS5.1
- begin to name flat shapes such as circle, triangle, square, rectangle ...   SS5.3, 5.4
- use a variety of shapes to make models, pictures and patterns
  and describe them   SS5.2, 5.4, 5.5

Talk about, recognise and recreate patterns: for example, simple repeating
or symmetrical patterns in the environment (see also Reasoning)   SS5.5, 6.1

Use everyday words to describe position, direction and movement:
for example, follow and give instructions about positions, directions and
movements in P.E. and other activities
- positions   SS6.2
- directions   SS6.3, 6.5
- movements   SS6.4, 6.5

About Cambridge Mathematics Direct

What is Cambridge Mathematics Direct?

Cambridge Mathematics Direct provides everything you need to plan, teach and assess your daily maths lesson in a simple, manageable way.

Cambridge Mathematics Direct is in line with the recommendations of the National Numeracy Strategy and places a strong emphasis on whole-class teaching, oral and mental work and direct communication with pupils. It directly reflects the philosophy and content of the *Framework for teaching mathematics*, providing comprehensive coverage of the learning objectives for each year.

Learning objectives have been grouped into three strands within the Teacher's Handbook: *Counting and recognising numbers; Adding and subtracting*; and *Measures, shape and space*. Solving problems is included throughout. Each strand has been divided into mathematical **topics** consisting of **blocks of lessons** that provide total coverage of the learning objectives for the term. The following example shows how the strand *Counting and recognising numbers* is broken down. Each strand is broken down in a similar way.

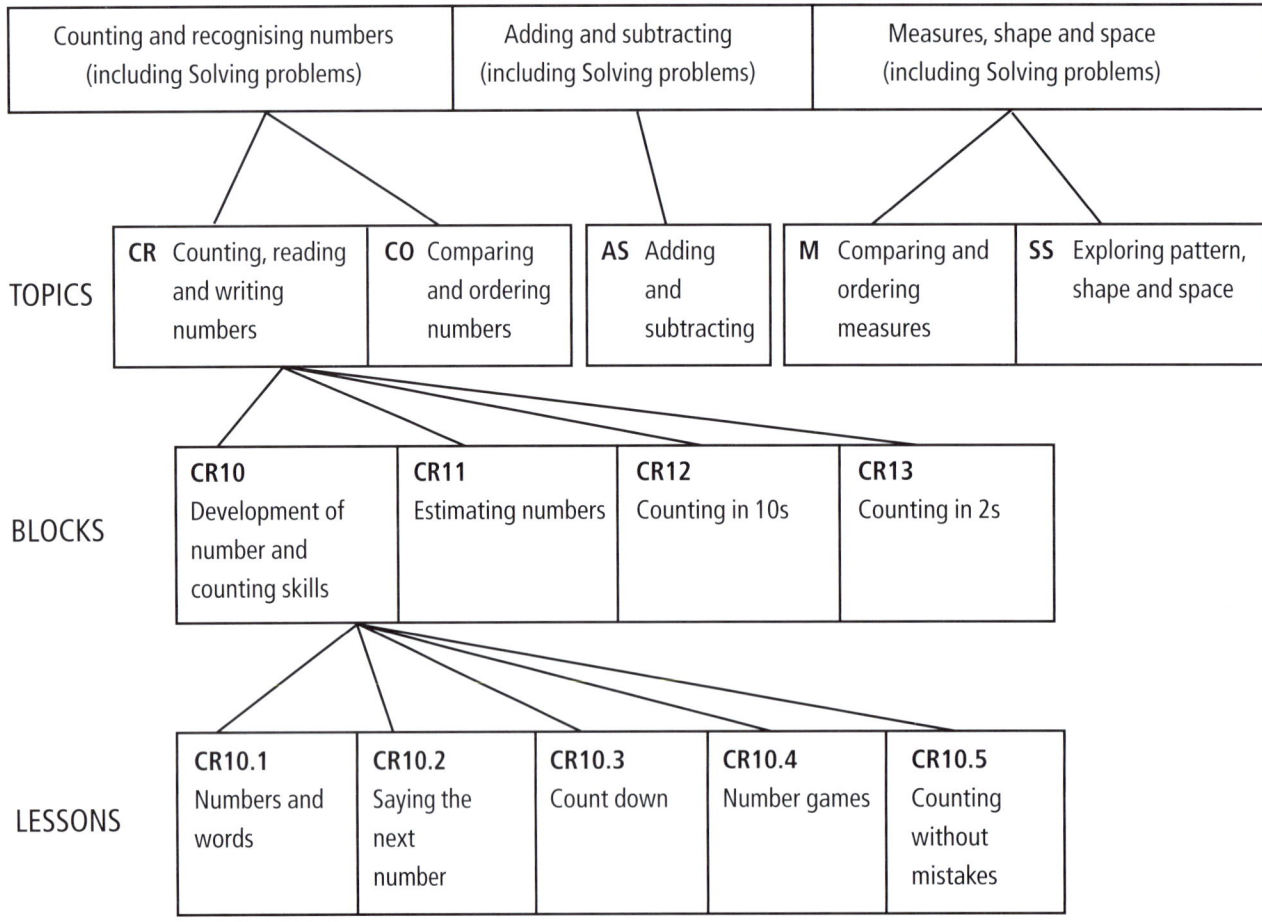

The numbering of blocks follows on from that in the Autumn/Spring Teacher's Handbook.

The materials in Cambridge Mathematics Direct R

Autumn/Spring	Summer
Teacher's Handbook	Teacher's Handbook
Activity Sheets	Activity Sheets
Handwriting Workbook	
Interactive Pictures	
Interactive Pictures User Guide	
Assess and Review Lesson Plans	
Maths Review Workbook	

Teacher's Handbooks

This Cambridge Mathematics Direct Summer Teacher's Handbook is organised in daily lesson plan format. This will begin to prepare pupils for the more structured lesson format they will encounter in Year 1. It contains the following sections:

1 Planning your daily maths lesson

Ideas on how to organise your daily maths lesson using the lesson plans in Cambridge Mathematics Direct. There is also a blueprint on pages 14–15 that explains the features of the plans.

2 Matching to the NNS Framework for teaching mathematics objectives

Cambridge Mathematics Direct R covers all the learning objectives for Reception in the *Framework for teaching mathematics/Early learning goals*. Concepts are covered at least once in the material. The matching grids on pages 7–9 show how lessons in *CMD Reception Summer Term* match to the *Framework*. Use it to find the learning objectives you are interested in.

3 Mental maths

Each lesson plan contains ideas for the oral and mental starter. When there are particular skills you want to concentrate on, you can substitute different activities. An Oral work and mental ideas bank has been provided for each strand, (see pp 30–33; 84–85 and 108–109). Refer to these sections when planning the oral and mental maths skills your class will focus on over a half-term.

4 Lesson plans

Lessons follow the three-part structure recommended by the National Numeracy Strategy: oral and mental warm-up, followed by the main teaching activity (direct teaching and pupil activities) and then the plenary to review the concepts covered by the lesson.

The lesson plans are arranged in blocks within the relevant maths topic. Each topic begins with an introduction to the key concepts covered in the blocks.

Activity Sheets

The photocopiable sheets can be used in a variety of ways:

- Several of the pages provide general resources (e.g. number tracks, number cards).
- Some sheets are integral to a particular lesson and have been written to be used by the whole class, or by children doing core, support or extension work. You can differentiate the activity or change it slightly if you want children to repeat it, by altering the range of numbers before photocopying.

Interactive Pictures

Some of the lessons in *CMD Reception* are based around interactive pictures. These A1-sized colour pictures prompt whole-class discussion and their content is related to the learning objectives for several lessons.

They are easy to use by clipping to an easel or fixing to a wall. Washable spirit pens may be used on their write-on, wipe-off surface.

Interactive Pictures User Guide

This guide further develops the use of the Interactive Pictures. It contains a wide variety of ideas and activities for use in the Oral/mental starter and whole class direct teaching. There is also a suggestion explaining how each interactive picture can be used as part of an interactive display. The guide relates to all topics covered in the *Framework for teaching mathematics/Early learning goals.*

Assessment

Short term assessment

Each lesson plan provides activities and questions in the **plenary** session. These will help you to monitor children's progress and identify misconceptions.

Medium term assessment

The *Assess and Review Lesson Plans* and *Maths Review Workbook* provide material for this purpose. The Assess and Review Lesson Plans relate to all the key objectives, with opportunities for whole class, group and individual assessment. The Maths Review Workbook provides additional recorded assessment.

Long term assessment

Information will be gathered throughout the year as a result of the above activities. It can be recorded on the key objectives record sheet provided in the planning pack.

Handwriting Workbook

This book focuses on the actual formation of numerals. It can be used at any point during the year, as appropriate.

Planning with Cambridge Mathematics Direct

The *Framework for teaching mathematics/Early learning goals* and the National Curriculum specify which learning objectives are to be covered in Reception. The order in which you teach these objectives will depend on your teaching plan for the year. You might be following the broad outline given by the half-termly plan in the *Framework,* your LEA's or school's scheme of work, or a plan that you have developed yourself. You can use Cambridge Mathematics Direct to follow all these plans. In addition, we suggest a specific order for teaching *Reception* which provides a logical progression of concepts.

When planning, decide which areas of maths you want to teach and select the block or blocks of lessons that cover these objectives. The order of lessons in a block has been chosen so that there is a sensible development and progression of concepts. You can even pick out individual lessons if you prefer, as lessons are independent of each other. Activities in one lesson do not call upon items prepared in a previous lesson (although you will need to make sure that children have the understanding necessary to be able to tackle the new concepts you want to teach).

Using the lesson plans

The lesson plans in the Cambridge Mathematics Direct Teacher's Handbooks have been provided as a starting point for the daily maths lesson but there is no need to follow them exactly. You could substitute activities that you have already found to be successful for those suggested.

There are several ways to use the lesson plans in Cambridge Mathematics Direct:

- You can dip in and out of the course choosing lessons where they fit in with the other resources you have in school.
- You can follow the half-termly plans suggested in the *Framework for teaching mathematics* and choose lessons from the planning grid that meet the objectives you are interested in.
- You can choose to teach complete blocks of lessons concentrating on one idea at a time.

The following is a suggested order for teaching the lessons in the *CMD Reception: Summer Teacher's Handbook.*

Summer	
CO3.1–3.5	More ordering and ordinal numbers
CR10.1–10.5	Development of number and counting skills
SS5.1–5.5	Investigating shapes
CR11.1–11.5	Estimating numbers
AS5.1–5.5	Counting on and counting back
CR12.1–12.3	Counting in 10s
CR13.1–13.5	Counting in 2s
SS6.1–6.5	Patterns and movement
M3.1–3.5	Time and comparing more than 2 measures
AS6.1–6.5	Adding and subtracting puzzles

Each lesson plan is arranged across a double-page spread. The blueprint on pages 14–15 explains what happens in each part of the lesson. It is not necessary to do everything in the lesson plan if you feel that some activities are not appropriate for the children in your class at that time. Questions for the teacher to ask are in italics.

Lesson structure

The structure of each lesson is in accordance with the recommendations of the National Numeracy Strategy. It provides a variety of approaches in the daily maths lesson and allows the concepts to be taught in the most suitable way.

Each lesson contains fully differentiated pupil activities. Activities suitable for children working at the level specified for their year are called 'core activities'. These practise and reinforce the concepts and skills taught during the direct teaching session.

Extension activities are included in every lesson. This work may be completed after the Core activity, or it may stand alone.

Some children need to revisit earlier work before they start something new. The Support activities (denoted by ★) provide this extra experience. It may also be appropriate for some children to revisit activities from the Autumn/Spring Teacher's Handbook and Activity Sheets, before they are ready for the Summer Term activities.

Each lesson suggests levels of support for each activity. One of the activities will always be adult-led, with focused questioning from the teacher. Another will be adult-supported, the intention being that either the teacher or another adult will supprt the children's work in this activity. The third activity will be independent. A balance of support is provided across the block, to allow children opportunities both for adult support, and to experience independent work.

How the daily lesson plans work

These major objectives for the lesson relate directly to the *Framework for teaching mathematics*.

A list of equipment required. This includes any Interactive Picture (IP) and Activity Sheet (AS) to be used.

This is the main purpose of the lesson, which pupils can then focus on in the Plenary.

Key words are taken from the *NNS Mathematical vocabulary* relevant to the lesson.

These are warm-up activities that focus on rapid recall of number facts and mental strategies.

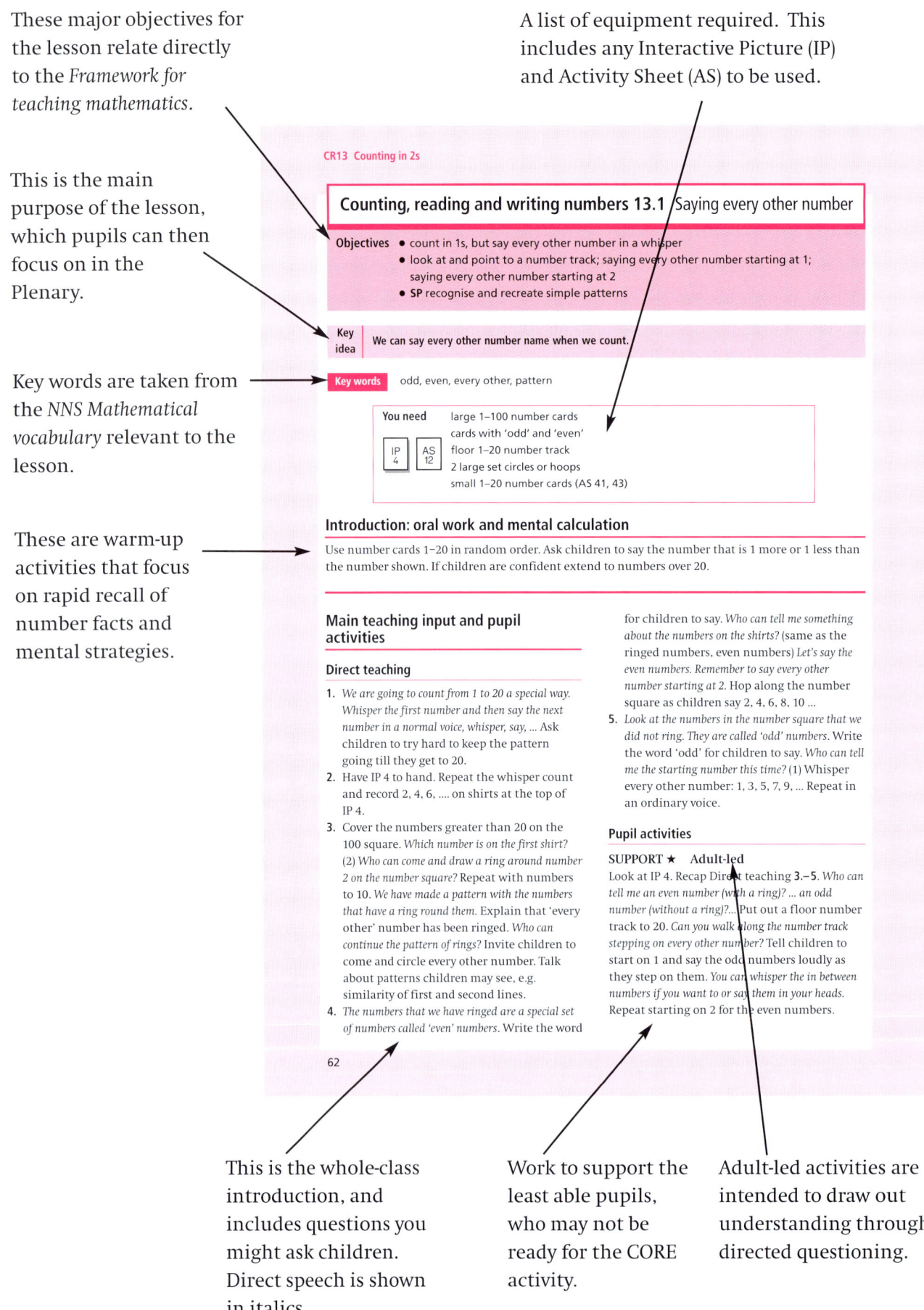

CR13 Counting in 2s

Counting, reading and writing numbers 13.1 / Saying every other number

Objectives
- count in 1s, but say every other number in a whisper
- look at and point to a number track; saying every other number starting at 1; saying every other number starting at 2
- **SP** recognise and recreate simple patterns

Key idea We can say every other number name when we count.

Key words odd, even, every other, pattern

You need large 1–100 number cards
cards with 'odd' and 'even'
floor 1–20 number track
2 large set circles or hoops
small 1–20 number cards (AS 41, 43)
IP 4 AS 12

Introduction: oral work and mental calculation

Use number cards 1–20 in random order. Ask children to say the number that is 1 more or 1 less than the number shown. If children are confident extend to numbers over 20.

Main teaching input and pupil activities

Direct teaching

1. *We are going to count from 1 to 20 a special way. Whisper the first number and then say the next number in a normal voice, whisper, say, …* Ask children to try hard to keep the pattern going till they get to 20.
2. Have IP 4 to hand. Repeat the whisper count and record 2, 4, 6, …. on shirts at the top of IP 4.
3. Cover the numbers greater than 20 on the 100 square. *Which number is on the first shirt?* (2) *Who can come and draw a ring around number 2 on the number square?* Repeat with numbers to 10. *We have made a pattern with the numbers that have a ring round them.* Explain that 'every other' number has been ringed. *Who can continue the pattern of rings?* Invite children to come and circle every other number. Talk about patterns children may see, e.g. similarity of first and second lines.
4. *The numbers that we have ringed are a special set of numbers called 'even' numbers.* Write the word

for children to say. *Who can tell me something about the numbers on the shirts?* (same as the ringed numbers, even numbers) *Let's say the even numbers. Remember to say every other number starting at 2.* Hop along the number square as children say 2, 4, 6, 8, 10 …

5. *Look at the numbers in the number square that we did not ring. They are called 'odd' numbers.* Write the word 'odd' for children to say. *Who can tell me the starting number this time?* (1) Whisper every other number: 1, 3, 5, 7, 9, … Repeat in an ordinary voice.

Pupil activities

SUPPORT ★   Adult-led
Look at IP 4. Recap Direct teaching **3.–5.** *Who can tell me an even number (with a ring)? … an odd number (without a ring)?…* Put out a floor number track to 20. *Can you walk along the number track stepping on every other number?* Tell children to start on 1 and say the odd numbers loudly as they step on them. *You can whisper the in between numbers if you want to or say them in your heads.* Repeat starting on 2 for the even numbers.

62

This is the whole-class introduction, and includes questions you might ask children. Direct speech is shown in italics.

Work to support the least able pupils, who may not be ready for the CORE activity.

Adult-led activities are intended to draw out understanding through directed questioning.

CORE activities are aimed at the average ability pupils and focus on key skills and concepts.

A teacher or other available adult provides support in understanding the activity and drawing out the key concepts and skills.

Work to extend and challenge the most able pupils.

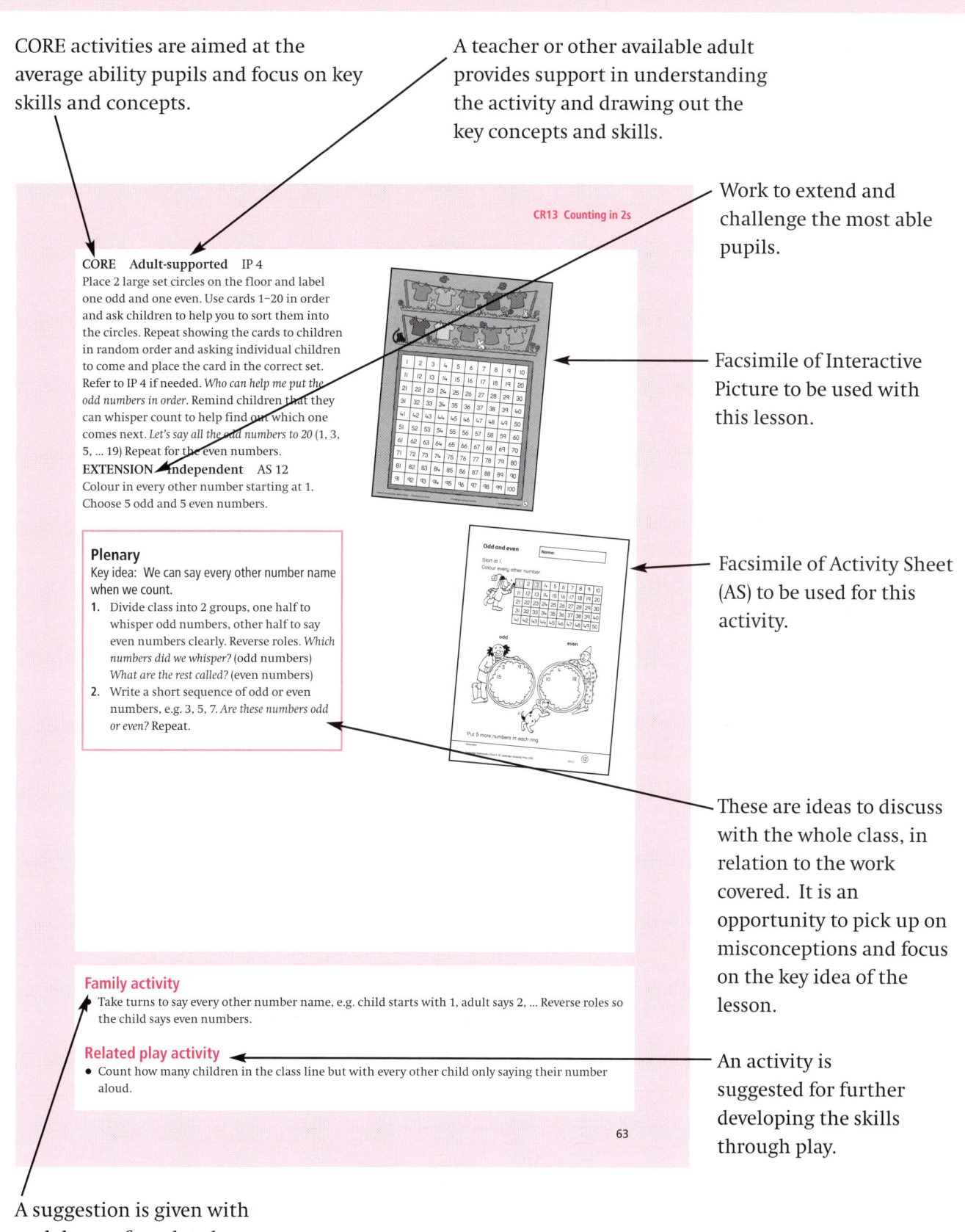

CR13 Counting in 2s

CORE   Adult-supported   IP 4
Place 2 large set circles on the floor and label one odd and one even. Use cards 1–20 in order and ask children to help you to sort them into the circles. Repeat showing the cards to children in random order and asking individual children to come and place the card in the correct set. Refer to IP 4 if needed. *Who can help me put the odd numbers in order.* Remind children that they can whisper count to help find out which one comes next. *Let's say all the odd numbers to 20* (1, 3, 5, ... 19) Repeat for the even numbers.
EXTENSION   Independent   AS 12
Colour in every other number starting at 1. Choose 5 odd and 5 even numbers.

Plenary
Key idea: We can say every other number name when we count.
1. Divide class into 2 groups, one half to whisper odd numbers, other half to say even numbers clearly. Reverse roles. *Which numbers did we whisper?* (odd numbers) *What are the rest called?* (even numbers)
2. Write a short sequence of odd or even numbers, e.g. 3, 5, 7. *Are these numbers odd or even?* Repeat.

Family activity
Take turns to say every other number name, e.g. child starts with 1, adult says 2, ... Reverse roles so the child says even numbers.

Related play activity
• Count how many children in the class line but with every other child only saying their number aloud.

63

Facsimile of Interactive Picture to be used with this lesson.

Facsimile of Activity Sheet (AS) to be used for this activity.

These are ideas to discuss with the whole class, in relation to the work covered. It is an opportunity to pick up on misconceptions and focus on the key idea of the lesson.

An activity is suggested for further developing the skills through play.

A suggestion is given with each lesson for related activities the children could do at home.

Interactive maths displays

Children can benefit greatly from having access to a display they can use to extend their mathematical experiences, either as part of the lesson or in their own time. The main purpose of any display should be to support teaching and learning, to share learning with others and to celebrate achievement. The teacher should also try to provide opportunities for children to experience mathematics through a variety of learning styles, such as visual, aural and kinaesthetic.

Setting up a display

- Ideally a display should contain work done by the teacher and by children. Small whiteboards can be useful to allow children to make spontaneous contributions to a display.
- Interactive displays should be wholly accessible to children and thus need to be hard-wearing enough to allow them to move pieces, handle equipment, etc.
- An interactive display should provide opportunities for children to explore mathematical ideas independently. By using it to model concepts during maths lessons you can help to encourage independent use. When planning your display, therefore, you should consider how it can be used with the whole class, small groups, and individuals.
- A display should include relevant mathematical vocabulary as well as questions and activities to stimulate children's thinking.
- Encouraging children to talk about what they are doing with an interactive display can help them to develop mathematical language.

Ideas for a table-top display

You need
10 different sized toy frogs
2 'logs'
a 'pond'
1–10 number cards

1–10 number name cards
picture cards of 1–10 frogs
individual white boards and pens
Labels:
'Put some frogs in the pond.',
'how many?', 'how many left?', 'count',
'more', 'fewer', 'Draw your picture here.'

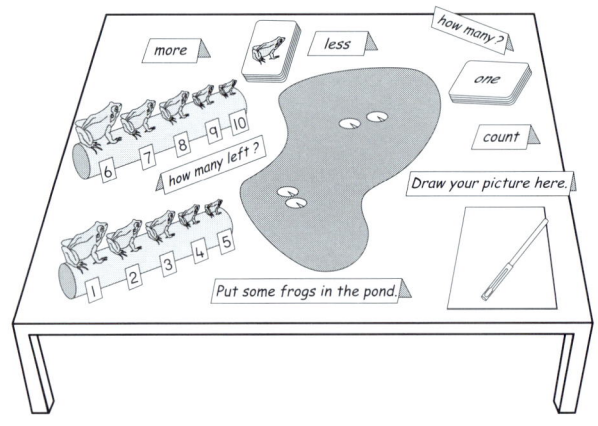

Possible questions
Can you put 5 frogs in the pond? If you put 2 more frogs in the pond, how many are there altogether? How many frogs are left on the log? Can you find the number 3? Can you find the number that matches this number name/picture card? Can you put these numbers/number names/picture cards in order? Can you put these frogs in order of height?
Less able: you could use activities that focus on number recognition.
More able: you could ask children to predict answers before checking, e.g. *If there were 7 frogs in the pond, how many would be left on the logs?* A problem solving activity could also be used, e.g. *How many ways can you put 4 frogs on the 2 logs?*

Adaptations
- Include balances so children can compare masses of frogs.
- Include a simple board game where children throw a dice and move a small frog along stepping stones towards a lily pad.
- A display should allow children to consolidate previous learning, but opportunities can also be included to extend children's thinking. Problem solving can be encouraged by asking children to investigate a question or statement, e.g. *How many ways can you put the 4 frogs on the 2 logs?*

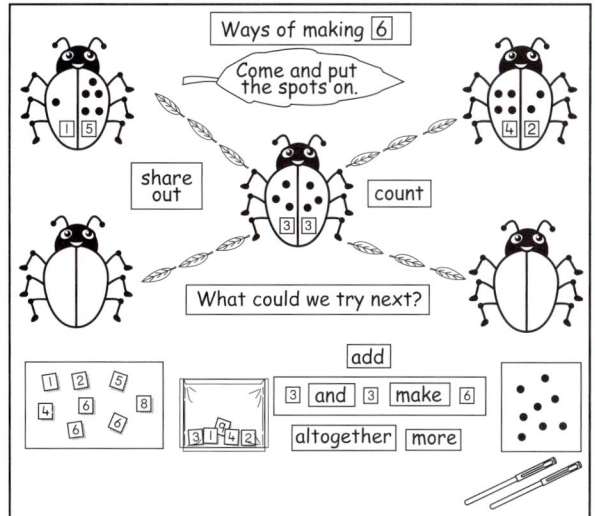

- Activities provided by a display need to reflect the range of learning needs in your class. For instance you may encourage one group of children to compare the sizes of 2 objects or numbers, while another group compares and orders a larger set.
- The context of your display should be meaningful to your children and could be chosen to reflect other areas of the curriculum, e.g. the local environment, stories, rhymes, etc.
- Displays need to build on children's experiences both at home and at school and aspects included might reflect the cultural diversity in the class, e.g. multi-cultural dolls, fabric patterns, food, etc.
- Displays need to be changed regularly to reflect current work in the classroom. By varying the style of your displays and the types of activities they include, you can help to promote children's interest in mathematics.
- Having mathematics displayed effectively, attributes value and status to the subject and helps to raise parents' awareness of the importance of mathematical experiences in the early years. It should aim to celebrate children's work, to raise their confidence and self-esteem.
- Links with home can be developed, by encouraging children to bring things into school to form part of a display. Displays can also give ideas to parents about how they can develop their child's mathematical thinking at home.

Ideas for a wall display

You need
sets of 0–10 number cards
counters
2 clear plastic pockets
5 laminated ladybirds
2 blank laminated cards
pens
Blu-Tack
Labels:
(fixed to display) 'Ways of making □', 'Come and put the spots on.', 'count', 'share out', 'What could we try next?'
(laminated and moveable) 'add', 'and', 'altogether' 'more', 'make'

Possible questions
How many 6s can you see? Can you draw a total of 5 spots on each ladybird? How many more spots do you need if you put 2 spots on one side? Can you use cards (and write numbers) to make a sentence for this ladybird? Can you write (find the number card for) the number of spots on this side?
Less able: children could share out the appropriate number of counters, rather than drawing spots. You may want to focus on making numbers to 5.
More able: you could ask children to find 2 number cards that make a given total and then to demonstrate why by drawing spots. Children could find and record all the different ways of making a given total.

Adaptations
- Change the focus to investigating 'What happens when you add ... ?', e.g. *Put some spots on 1 side of a ladybird. How many are there? How many would there be if you added 2 more?*
- Change the focus of the display to subtraction, e.g. *Put 6 spots on each ladybird. How many would be left if you took away 1 ... 2 ... 3 ... 4?*

Using the indoor environment

Reception classrooms are full of opportunities for children to develop and consolidate mathematical language and concepts through play activities. Included in this section are suggestions for activities that children can undertake in play areas, as well as some that can be used with the whole class or as part of daily routines. Most of the activities can easily be adapted to suit a range of contexts and the abilities of your children.

Preparing the classroom environment

General displays can be useful to promote mathematical learning. Try to include:

- a display area dedicated to the week's topics, incorporating appropriate mathematical language and children's work
- a permanent number display of resources used regularly (numbers 0 to 20, a blank number track, a number square, ...)
- an area to display the current IP
- a wall display/poster of flat shapes in a variety of colours and sizes (circles, triangles, squares, rectangles, stars)
- a table area making equipment relating to the week's topics easily accessible to children (e.g. balances, 3-D shapes, objects/containers of different sizes, number jigsaws, objects and sorting trays, counting objects)
- numbers or different coloured shapes to identify coat hooks, tables ...
- picture borders around display boards to provide opportunities for counting objects
- notices and labels that involve numbers, e.g. a notice showing how many children can play in the sand at any one time, a label showing how many cars belong in a box
- appropriate timers to limit how long is spent on activities, e.g. using computer, tidying away

Indoor activities

Counting

- Use a malleable material such as clay:
  To make a given number of items,
  e.g. *Make 5 cakes.*
  To make/continue an indented line of repeating pattern.
- Use sand:
  Bury objects and ask children to find given numbers of particular items, e.g. *Find 6 red buttons and 4 yellow buttons.*
  Ask one child to hide a given number of objects and another child to find them all.
  Give children a number of flags and ask them to make a sandcastle for each.
- When children are using water:
  How many cubes can you put in the boat before it sinks or turns over?
  Ask them to catch a given number of magnetic fish.
- When using bricks:
  Define the number of bricks to be used, e.g. *Make a tower with 20 bricks.*
  How many bricks did you use to build your house?
- When using musical instruments ask children to:
  Count drum beats made by other children.
  Create a musical composition using a given number of drum beats.
  Use a given number of instruments to create a musical composition.
- Ask children to model number rhymes using props, e.g. '5 little ducks went swimming one day ...'
  Ask questions during registration time (or using self registering name cards), e.g. *How many boys are in class today? How many children are away from school today? How many children are having school lunch? Can we put everyone here today in pairs/groups of 5?*
- When children are in a class line:

Let's count forwards/backwards from … along the line.

Let's count forwards/backwards in 2s/10s from …

Reading and writing numbers

- By using number cards, many of the counting activities already listed can be adapted to give opportunities for number recognition, e.g. give children a number card: *I want you to find this many blue buttons in the sand. Find the number card that matches how many cubes you can put in the boat before it sinks.*
- When children are using sand:
  Ask them to trace given numbers in the sand/ trace numbers in the sand for other children to identify.
  Hide plastic numbers in the sand and ask, e.g. *Can you find the number 2?*
- When children are in the book corner:
  Find page number 12 in your book.
  Find a picture of a squirrel in this book and write down which page it is on.

Comparing and ordering numbers

- When children are using water:
  Ask them to fish for magnetic numbers in order from 0 to 10.
  Ask them to order 4 or 5 magnetic numbers they have caught .
- When children are using bricks:
  Ask 2 children to compare the numbers of bricks they have used: *Who used more/fewer bricks?*
  Ask them to use a number of bricks in a given range, e.g. *Make a tower using between 5 and 10 bricks.*
  Show a tower. *I want you to make a tower using 1 more/less brick than I have used.*
- Practise using ordinal numbers in a class line, e.g. *Who is seventh in the line? Who is between the third and fifth person in the line? Where are you in the line? Where is Alisha in the line?*

Adding and subtracting

- Ask children to collect 2 numbers that make a given total by finding plastic numbers buried in sand or by fishing for magnetic numbers.
- Ask children to model and solve number story problems using toys:

There are 5 dolls in the dolls' house. How many more do you need to make 8 altogether?

Put some dolls in the kitchen and some in the lounge so there are 7 dolls altogether.

There are 10 dinosaurs in the forest, 3 are drinking from the river. How many are not drinking?

Choose dinosaurs that stand on 4 legs. How many legs do 3 of them have?

Reasoning about numbers or shapes

- When children are in a classroom post office ask them to:
  Choose a piece of brown paper big enough to wrap a given parcel.
  Choose a suitably sized box to send a given present in.
  Sort stamps/parcels into groups.
  Estimate, and then check, how many coins there are in the till.
  Arrange a given number of stamps on a parcel in a repeating pattern.
  Challenge them to share a given number of stamps between 2 parcels in different ways.
- When children are using water:
  Ask them to predict, then check, how many cubes a boat will hold. *What about 2 boats? Find out how many trips the boat will need to make to take all these cubes from one side of the water tray to the other?*
- When using musical instruments, ask children to make a composition with a pattern of sounds:
  Using pauses, e.g. ting, ting, pause, ting, ting, pause … on a triangle
  Using volume of sound, e.g. loud, soft, loud, soft … on a tambourine
  Using tempo, e.g. 5 slow beats, 5 fast beats, 5 slow beats, 5 fast beats … on a drum
- When children are using the book corner:
  Ask children to sort some books according to their content, e.g. putting all animal books together. *Put all the books taller than this one on the bottom shelf.*

Problems involving 'real life' or money

- When children are baking biscuits:
  Ask them to make their mixture into a given number of biscuits.
  Put a measured amount of 1 ingredient (e.g. 2 spoonfuls) into the mixing bowl and ask a

child to add double the amount of another ingredient.
Ask children to share a given number of decorations equally between their biscuits.

- When children are using a classroom shop:
Ask them to find which things they can pay for exactly using one coin.
Ask them to 'buy' items by selecting suitable coins.
Ask a 'shopkeeper' to give any change that is needed.

Comparing and ordering measures

- When children are using sand:
How many cups of sand fill the bottle?
Will all the sand from the bottle fit into this bucket?
Which of these containers holds the most?
Find out how much sand will balance 5 bricks.

- When children are playing with suitable toys:
Find a dinosaur longer/shorter/taller/heavier/lighter than this one.
Which is the longest/shortest/tallest/heaviest/lightest dinosaur in this group?
Which 2 dinosaurs together measure about the same as this one?

- When baking:
Make a biscuit about the same size as this one.
Ask children to balance ingredients against an egg.
Ask children to stir the mixture for a set amount of time, e.g. for as long it takes for the sand to run through a timer, for a count of 10, for 6 stirs …
Ask children to investigate what they can achieve in a given time, e.g. *Who can make the longest paper chain before all the sand runs through the timer?*

- Play 'I spy' by comparing objects in the classroom: *I spy with my little eye something … higher/lower than the clock … wider/narrower than the door … taller/shorter than the desk … heavier/lighter than a chair … that holds more/less than this bucket …*

Exploring pattern, shape and space

- When children are using a malleable material:
Can you cut out different sized squares?
Can you cut out flat shapes with one curved side/only straight sides.

- When children are making models:
Give them instructions about the shapes they can use, e.g. *Use 8 big cubes, 2 small cubes and a cone.*
Ask them to describe to a friend how they made their model, e.g. *I put a large cube on the bottom, then I put a smaller cube on top of it …*

- Ask children to use/cut out paper shapes to make a picture/pattern:
You must only use shapes with straight edges.
Hide a triangle somewhere in your picture. Can a friend find it?
Make a symmetrical pattern.

- When children are printing ask them to:
Create a repeating pattern.
Print with the edge of a ruler to a pattern of straight lines.
Print curved line patterns using string.
Make a symmetrical pattern by painting on one half of a piece of paper and folding.
How many circles can you print on this circle of paper?

- When children are using sand:
Ask them to find shapes hidden in the sand, e.g. *Find a yellow rectangle.*
Ask them to trace out given shapes in the sand.

- When children are using musical instruments:
Ask them to sort a group of instruments, e.g. by shape, size.
Ask them to point to/hit different parts of instruments, e.g. the top, bottom, side, edge.

- Play 'I spy' using positions of objects in the classroom: *I spy with my little eye something … above/below the clock … on the left/right of the door … next to/opposite the board …*

- Have a treasure hunt, with children looking for shapes in objects and features of the classroom, e.g. *Can you touch a square?*

- Whilst in a class line ask children to create/continue a pattern:
Changing order so the line is, e.g. boy, girl, boy, girl …
Saying words/numbers, e.g. today, tomorrow, today, tomorrow …; 10, 11, 12, 10, 11, 12 …
Making sounds, e.g. clap, clap, stamp, clap, clap, stamp …

Using the outdoor environment

In Reception, we should aim to give children maximum exposure to a wide variety of learning experiences. The outdoor environment is a valuable resource, accessible to everyone, that can provide opportunities for mathematics not available indoors.

Many activities can make use of the space and features of school grounds, and playground markings (e.g. coloured shapes, numbers, caterpillar number tracks, 100 square, snakes and ladders board ...) can provide a useful outdoor resource. However, to help children relate mathematics to the real world, use should also be made of locations in the wider environment.

Obviously the activities described here do not form an exhaustive list, but most can easily be adapted to suit the settings available to you and the abilities of your children. Some of the activities previously listed in the 'Indoor environment' section are also suitable for use outdoors.

Outdoor activities

Counting

- Ask children to count things they can see around them:
  How many ducks can you see on the pond?
  How many children are playing on the climbing frame?
- Ask children to find or collect numbers of items:
  Collect 10 fallen leaves.
  Bring me 4 pebbles.
  I have hidden coins around the playground. Find 5 of them.
  Count out 6 bean seeds to plant in each pot.
- Play large dice games:
  One child throws a dice, and counts the dots: Children must jump that number of times.
  Give each child a number from 1 to 6. Throw the dice. If a child's number is thrown, they run to the other end of the playground and back.
- Play the 'Lifeboats' game:

All children are 'swimming in the sea'. You shout, e.g. *Man the lifeboats in 3s.* Children get into groups of 3 on a large paper lifeboat cut-out. *Are there any children left out?*

Reading and writing numbers

- Use numbered toys/objects in the playground:
  Ask children to park a numbered vehicle in a bay with a matching number.
  Children must choose the appropriate number card/say the appropriate number name to match the number of the toy they want to play with.
  Find as many beanbags as you can with a 2 on.
- Use painted or chalked numbers/number track/100 square on the ground. Ask children to stand on/by a given number.
- Ask children to draw numbers using chalk on the ground.
- Ask children to point out numbers/a particular number on a maths trail, e.g. on doors, price labels, car registration plates ...

Comparing and ordering numbers

- Ask children to park numbered toy vehicles in order.
- Use numbers sewn onto clothes from the lost property box. Put up a washing line at child height and ask them to peg on the clothes in order.
- Write numbers on the sides of boxes. (A4 photocopy paper boxes are ideal.) Ask children to stack the boxes in order.
- Create situations for children to use/interpret ordinal numbers to describe where things are:
  Where is the number 7 on this car number plate?
  Point to the second house we come to with a red door.

Adding and subtracting

- Set up 'role play' situations for children to practise adding and subtracting:
  Sit some children on a 'bus'. *How many are there on the bus?* Ask individuals to get on/off the 'bus'. *How many got on/off? How many are there on the bus now?*
  Ask some children driving toy cars to park in

a 'car park'. *How many cars are there in the car park? Ask individuals to drive their cars in/out of the car park. How many drove in/out? How many cars are there in the car park now?* Set up a teddy bear's picnic. *How many teddies/plates are there? How many more plates will we need so each teddy has a plate? How many more plates than teddies are there?*

Reasoning about numbers or shapes

- Ask children to sort objects, e.g.
  large toy cars according to colour
  a collection found on a woodland trail
  large dominoes.
- Use a variety of different shaped boxes. Ask children to fill them with different shaped objects. Children explore which shapes fit best inside others.
- Challenge children to arrange a number of objects (e.g. 6 shells found on the beach) into 2 groups in different ways.
- Make estimates before investigating:
  How many footsteps/strides do you think it is from the climbing frame to the roundabout?
  How many children do you think can sit on the bench? What about on 2 benches?

Problems involving 'real life' or money

- Use things children can see around them:
  How many wheels are there on 2 cars?
  How many legs are there on 2 ducks?
  How many people would there be on the swings if 2 went to play on the seesaw?
- Ask children to find coins that have been hidden around the playground:
  Find a 2p coin.
  Find 2 different silver coins.
  Find coins that make 5p.

Comparing and ordering measures

- Use comparison activities:
  Put pebbles in these 2 buckets so that the green bucket is heavier.
  Line up the pots so the sunflowers are in order of height.
  Which flower do you think will hold the most/least soil?
- Set up challenges and compare results:
  Who ran the fastest?
  Who has made the tallest tower?

After children have thrown beanbags ask:
Whose beanbag is close to/far away from us?
Who can use 10 jumps to get from A to B? Who can use 5 jumps? When did you have to use bigger jumps?

Exploring pattern and shape and space

- Use shapes painted or drawn on the ground. Ask children to stand on/by a particular shape, e.g. *Stand on the red square.*
- Discuss shapes children can see around them:
  What shape is the window? How many corners has it got?
  Can you find a sign that is a circle?
- Ask children to draw shapes using chalk on the ground.
- Ask children to describe or make patterns they can see around them, e.g. bricks in a wall, planks in a fence, railings …
- Give children instructions using positional language:
  Stand between 2 trees.
  Sit on the grass in front of me.
- Ask a child to pretend to be a robot. Others give instructions to guide them through a maze/obstacle course using language such as forwards, backwards, turn left, turn right.

Stories, rhymes and games in maths

Teaching mathematics within a context enables young children to access ideas at a higher level. Stories, rhymes, and games can give context and provide additional interest to mathematical learning. They also give opportunities for children to develop their mathematical vocabulary.

Stories

- It is possible to draw mathematical ideas from a range of published stories, including those suggested in the *Framework for teaching mathematics*.
- You could provide a context for a particular concept by creating your own story.
- Story illustrations can provide impromptu opportunities for maths, especially counting.
- Some stories can enable children to visualise concepts or predict from patterns.

- Mathematical ideas within a story can be made more accessible by using appropriate props.
- You can use number cards to show numerals relevant to a story.
- A story can be used to reflect the learning objectives for one lesson or it can be used as a theme for a range of concepts over a longer period of time.
- You can choose stories that reflect the cultural mix of your class.

Using a story
The following ideas are based on the traditional tale 'Goldilocks and the three bears'.

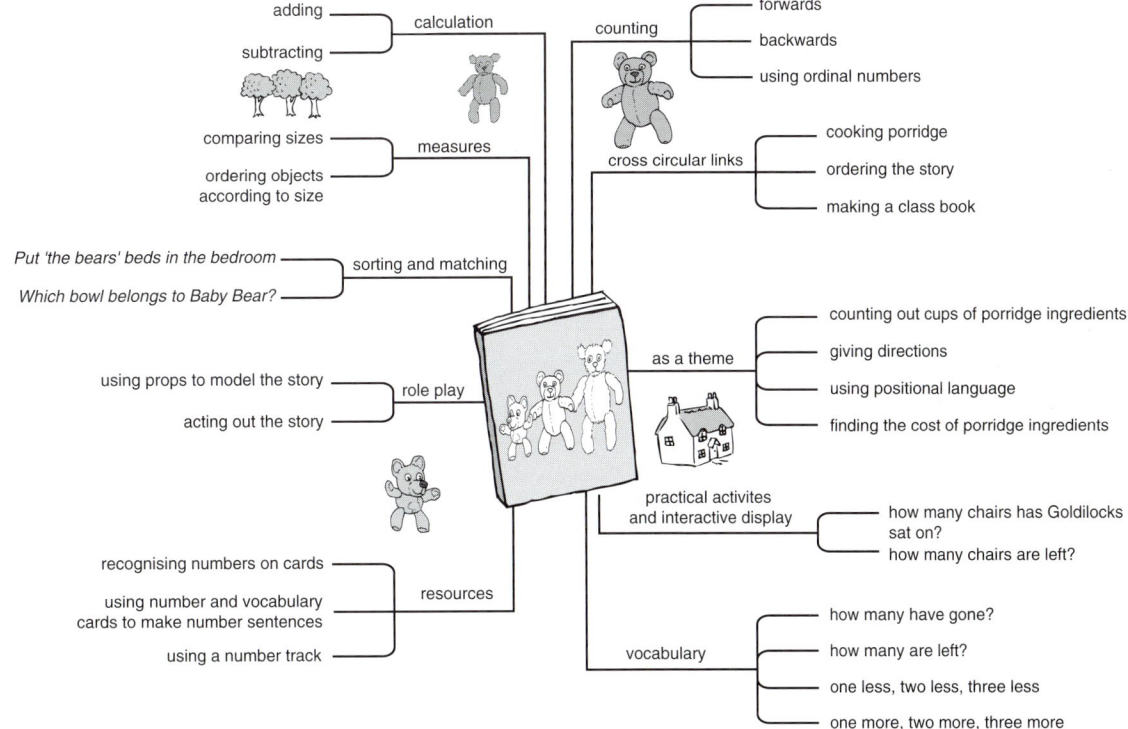

- A range of mathematical ideas can be developed directly through the story, e.g. counting, comparing and ordering the size of objects, sorting and matching, adding and subtracting.

- The story can also be used as a theme for other mathematical concepts, e.g. finding the cost of buying ingredients for making porridge from the class shop, counting out numbers of cups of each porridge ingredient, giving instructions to the three bears to direct them to Goldilocks, describing where objects are in the three bears' house ...

- Incorporating props can help children visualise concepts more easily, e.g. bears and a doll for Goldilocks; a house made using boxes for rooms; model bowls, chairs, beds ...
- You can make cross-curricular links, e.g. by cooking porridge, acting out the story, ordering pictures from the story, making a class book ...
- The story can be used as a theme for practical activities or an interactive class display.
- Resources can be used to help develop and record mathematical ideas, e.g. once 2 bowls of porridge have been eaten, you could ask children to find a number (or number name) card to match the number of bowls eaten ... to demonstrate finding the number of bowls of porridge left using a number track ... to use number and vocabulary cards to make a number sentence to show how many bowls of porridge are left (e.g. 3 take away 2 leaves 1).
- Mathematical vocabulary can be introduced to discussion about the story.

Rhymes

- Chanting rhymes allows children to learn concepts in an enjoyable manner.
- Whilst chanting in a group, children are supported by others, allowing them to learn with confidence.
- There are many rhymes that relate to counting on, e.g. '1, 2, 3, 4, 5, Once I caught a fish alive'. You should also aim to use rhymes covering other concepts, e.g. counting back, counting in 2s, shape names, telling the time ...
- Counting rhymes can help you to teach the concept of zero.
- Some traditional nursery rhymes (e.g. 'Sing a song of sixpence') provide opportunities for discussion about numbers and many (e.g. 'Jack and Jill went up the hill') can be used to consolidate positional language.
- You can select rhymes that reflect the cultural mix in your class.
- Rhymes can be used in the oral or mental starter, as an introduction to a lesson or as part of the plenary to reinforce the concepts introduced earlier.

Using a rhyme

The following ideas are based on the rhyme 'Seven dizzy dragons' from *Seven Dizzy Dragons and other maths rhymes*. Cambridge University Press 1997.

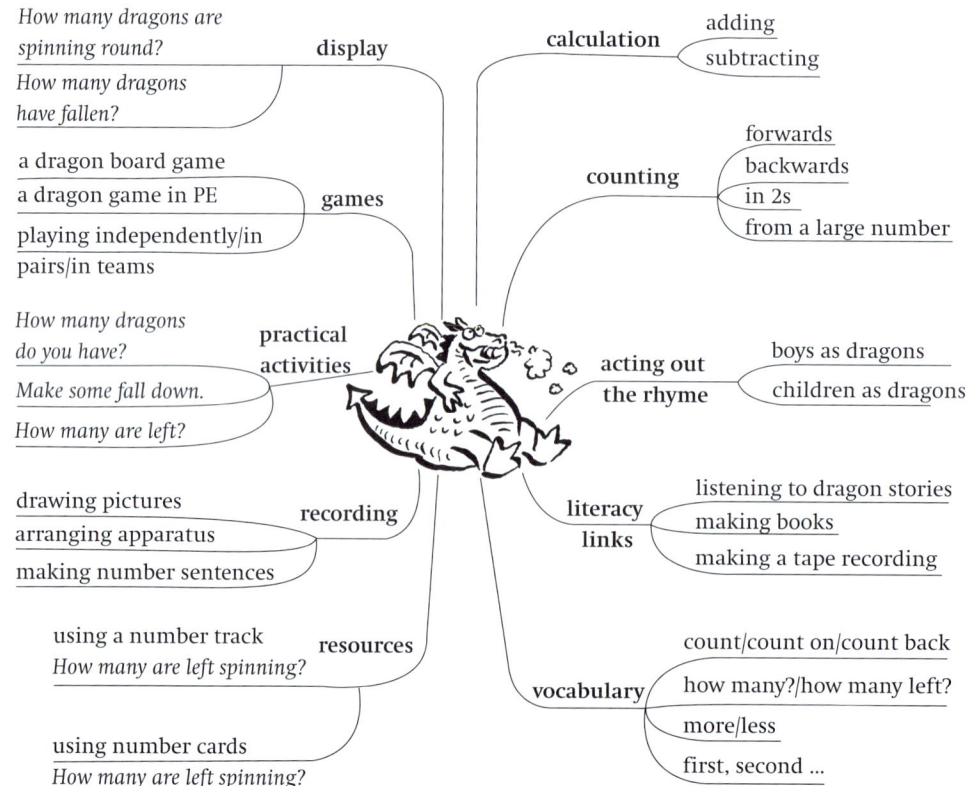

- Adapt the words in the rhyme so that the numbers count on.
- Introduce other ideas, e.g. counting back in 2s, starting from a larger number.
- Use supporting resources, e.g. toy dragons, children acting as dragons, number cards, a number track ...
- By using props the two groups of dragons (those spinning and those on the ground) can help children relate counting back to subtracting or counting on to adding.
- The dragon theme can be incorporated into practical activities, games and displays.
- The rhyme can be linked to literacy, e.g. by making books, recording and listening to the rhyme on a cassette, listening to stories about dragons ...
- The rhyme provides a context for work on recording. Children can draw pictures, arrange practical apparatus or use number and word cards to make simple number sentences (e.g. 7 take away 1 leaves 6).
- Mathematical vocabulary can be introduced into discussion about the rhyme.

Possible sources of rhymes

Gill Budgell and Kate Ruttle, *Big Book of Number Rhymes* (Cambridge University Press 2001)
Anita Straker, *Talking Points in Mathematics* (Cambridge University Press 1993), pp. 31–6
Sue Atkinson, Sharon Harrison and Lynne McClure, *Seven Dizzy Dragons and other maths rhymes* (Cambridge University Press 1997)
Anita Straker, *Mental Maths for Ages 5–7, Teacher's Book* (Cambridge University Press 1996), p. 7

Useful resources for games

Large and small dice (blank, dotted, numbered, money, different numbers of faces)
Spinners
Cards (spots, numbers, pictures, money, shapes)
Dominoes
'Coins'
Game boards and tracks
Counters and counting toys

Using tracks and grids

Children can progress from filling blank tracks/grids, to counting along blank and then numbered tracks/grids.

Games

- Games are an effective way of developing mathematical language and consolidating counting skills in a non-threatening atmosphere.
- The theme of a game can link with other areas of the curriculum.
- Games provide opportunities for children to develop their social skills by playing against a partner or as part of a team.
- Games can be used in the indoor or outdoor environment.
- Play traditional playground games, which incorporate mathematics, with children, e.g. counting in 'Hide and seek', choosing numbers in order in 'Hopscotch'.
- Games can be a good way of developing home–school links although it is advisable to send games home only if they have already been played at school.

Independent games

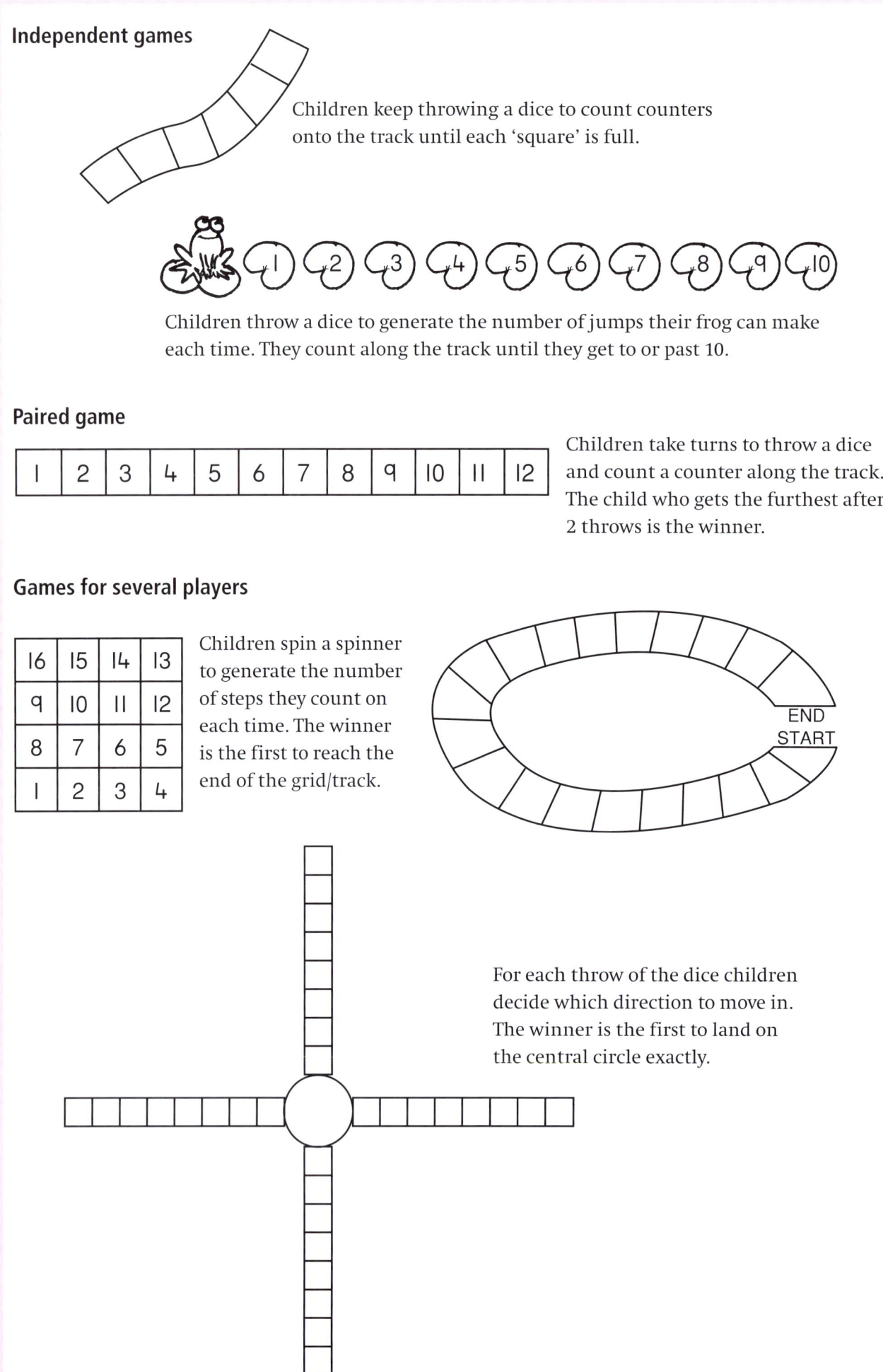

Children keep throwing a dice to count counters onto the track until each 'square' is full.

Children throw a dice to generate the number of jumps their frog can make each time. They count along the track until they get to or past 10.

Paired game

I	2	3	4	5	6	7	8	9	10	II	12

Children take turns to throw a dice and count a counter along the track. The child who gets the furthest after 2 throws is the winner.

Games for several players

16	15	14	13
9	10	II	12
8	7	6	5
I	2	3	4

Children spin a spinner to generate the number of steps they count on each time. The winner is the first to reach the end of the grid/track.

END
START

For each throw of the dice children decide which direction to move in. The winner is the first to land on the central circle exactly.

Use of resources in context

Appropriate use of resources can support children in a variety of ways by providing:
- opportunities for groups of children or the whole class to be taught together and all take part
- visual representations that can help development of mental strategies
- access to activities for children with English as an additional language
- opportunities for children to model and demonstrate particular concepts

Number tracks

Number tracks consist of sequential numbers written in spaces between lines (as opposed to number lines where numbers correspond to lines). Examples include number cards arranged on a washing line or held by a row of children, the counting stick, a line of numbered carpet tiles, game boards and some rulers. Blank number tracks can also be a useful resource.

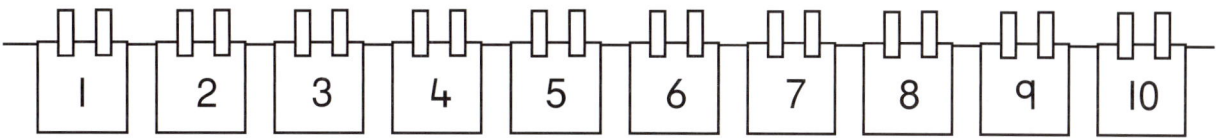

Number tracks are useful to help children visualise mathematical ideas about:
- counting on and back in 1s and 2s
- comparing numbers
- ordering numbers
- finding 1 more or 1 less
- finding a number between 2 given numbers
- adding and subtracting

Examples of number track activities
- Play 'What is my number': *My number is 1 more than 6 ... is smaller than 3 ... comes after 6 and before 9 ...*
- Place numbers on a track that is partially or completely blank.
- Ask children to use a number track to demonstrate why 1 of 2 numbers is greater/smaller and to give a number that lies between them.
- When playing board games, ask children to move 1 space more/less than the number they throw. *What number do you need to throw to get to the end?*

Number grids

Number grids are sequential numbers arranged in a grid. You might use all of a 1–100 (or 0–99) square, or a small part of one, e.g. 1–20.

1	2	3	4	5	6	7	8	9	10
11	12	13	14	15	16	17	18	19	20
21	22	23	24	25	26	27	28	29	30
31	32	33	34	35	36	37	38	39	40
41	42	43	44	45	46	47	48	49	50
51	52	53	54	55	56	57	58	59	60
61	62	63	64	65	66	67	68	69	70
71	72	73	74	75	76	77	78	79	80
81	82	83	84	85	86	87	88	89	90
91	92	93	94	95	96	97	98	99	100

Number grids can help to develop the same mathematical concepts as number tracks, but are also useful for:
- talking about patterns and making predictions
- counting in 10s

Examples of number grid activities
- Count forwards and backwards in 10s starting from different multiples of 10, and discuss patterns on a number square. *What comes just after/before 60 when we count in 10s?*
- Count in 2s, alternately whispering and 'shouting' and colouring the whispered numbers on a number grid. *Can you see the pattern? Do you think that we will shout number 13? Why?*

Number cards

Number cards consist of numerals on cards. A set can take the form of a fan or might include numbers represented in pictures or words.

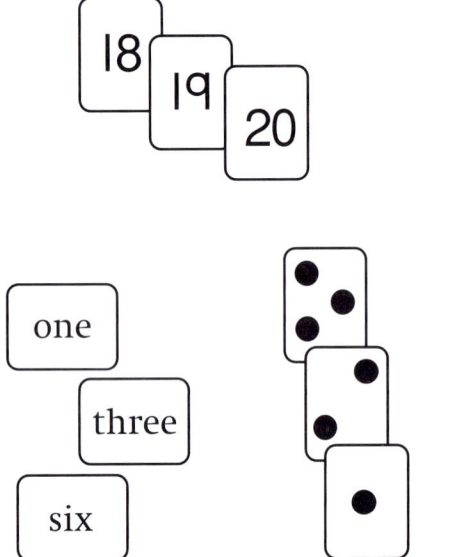

Number cards are especially useful in allowing children to show numerical answers to a range of questions (e.g. when comparing, ordering, adding or subtracting) and for generating problems in individual activities.

Examples of number card activities

- Order and compare numbers: *Can you put your 3 cards in order?*
- Show answers to closed questions: *If I had 3 pencils and then Jo gave me another one, how many would I have altogether? What is 1 less than 5?*
- Show possible answers to open questions: *Can you show me a number that is more than 7?*
- Generate additions and subtractions: *Choose 2 number cards. Add the numbers together ... Take the smaller number from the larger number.*

Dice

There are many different kinds of dice. The number of faces can vary and they can show, e.g. spots, numerals, shapes, colours, amounts of money.

Dice are especially useful for individual activities and games. They can help to consolidate:

- recognition of numerals
- counting
- simple addition and subtraction
- shape and colour recognition

Examples of dice activities

Ask children to roll a dice and:

- repeat an action that many times, e.g. jump on the spot
- take that many objects: *Who can collect 10 counters first?*
- find the number card that matches the number of spots
- add/subtract 1 to see how many spaces to move in a board game

Ask children to roll 2 dice and:

- move that number of spaces in a board game.

Equipment needed

The equipment needed is specified in each lesson plan. The following are a few things that it would be useful to have at all times.

- vocabulary cards[1]
- digit cards, 0–9[1] (one set per child)
- packs of number cards, 0–100[1]
- dice and spinners[1] especially 1–6 and blank dice[1]
- a variety of number tracks[1]. You could use IP 3 and IP 8 and AS 46–48.
- number squares[1]. You could use IP 4.
- counting stick
- counters[1] and interlocking cubes
- selections of different counting objects (e.g. small bears, shells, fir cones, farm animals ...)
- plastic coins
- dominoes[1]

[1] Available from BEAM 020 7684 3323

ORAL AND MENTAL IDEAS BANKS

and

LESSON PLANS

Numbers: oral work and mental calculation ideas bank

Use these short activities with the whole class or groups to practise and develop oral and mental maths skills. You can use them to supplement or replace the activities suggested in the Teacher's Handbook, or whenever you have a spare 5 minutes. Adapt activities so that they enable children to practise and apply concepts they have already covered. Whenever possible, allow time for children to share their ideas and strategies.

Try to vary the ways children respond to questions. You could ask them to give a 'thumbs up' signal when they are ready to answer, to limit distraction to those who are still thinking. They could use their fingers to show the answer. When appropriate, you could provide all children with a set of number cards with which to answer questions. You may want to ask children to wait for a signal from you before they show their answers. You could ask children to discuss ideas with a partner before they share them with the rest of the group.

Discussing numbers in context

- *What numbers do you know? Where have you seen them or used them?* e.g. ages, number of brothers and sisters, door numbers, ...
- *Who has a birthday today? How old are you? Show your age on your fingers. Clap your age.*

Saying and using number names in order

- Count around a circle, with children taking turns to say the next number. When numbers get too large, restart the count or count backwards.
- Vary the way children recite numbers in order, e.g. *Let's do it in a whisper ... very slowly/quickly.*
- Play 'What's gone wrong?'. Say number names 'in order' but including errors, e.g. miss out a number, reverse 2 numbers. Children call out when they notice an error and describe what has gone wrong.
- *Count in your head until I say stop. What number did you reach? Now count out loud to show me how you counted.*

Recognising numerals

- Place a set of numbered birthday cards in order (1–5 or beyond).

Children say each number as you point to it. *Come and take the card with 5 on ...*
- *Show me the number 4 using your fingers/with cubes/on the number track/by writing it in the air ...*
- Without children seeing, pick a large number card. Cover the numeral with a piece of card and then slowly uncover it, stopping frequently to ask: *What number do you think it could be?* Eventually reveal the number to check. Uncover numerals in different directions, e.g. from top to bottom, left to right ...

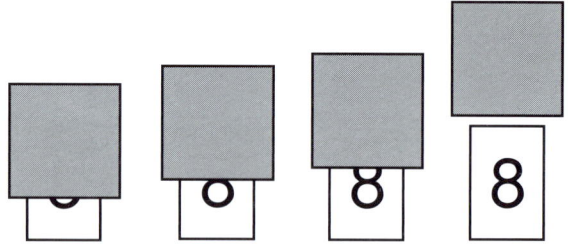

0, 3, 5, 6, 8? ... 6, 8? ... must be 8 ...   it is!
- Play bingo games.
  Vary how numbers are presented on cards.

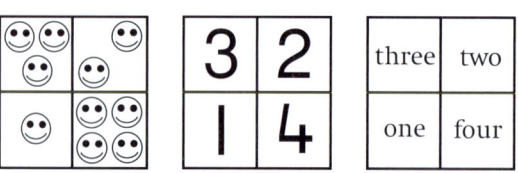

Vary how numbers are called, e.g. say them, show a number card, use fingers, show a collection of objects.
- Display a collection of numbered items. *Which teddy has 4 on it? Which car has 6 on it?*

Counting objects

- *Count these cubes* (all the same size and shape). *Now count these bricks* (different sizes and shapes).
- Give each child some coloured beads. *Make a pattern with your beads and count them to see how many you have. Now make a different pattern and count again. How many are there now?*
- Arrange a few counters in a line. *How many counters are there?* Move the counters into a random arrangement. *Count them again. You can touch them, but you mustn't move them.* Rearrange the counters again. *This time you must count them without touching them. How many are there?*
- Show a vertical tower of interlocking cubes. *Count the cubes.* Turn the tower to a horizontal position. *How many cubes now?* Split the tower apart, placing the cubes in a line. *Now how many cubes are there?* Rearrange the cubes randomly and count again.
- *I've got some oranges. Who can count them? I'd like to buy 3 bananas. Who can count out the right number for me?*
- Count numbers of different items. Discuss strategies for making sure each object is counted just once, e.g. arranging items in a line.
- Make a set of cards with spots on, some in orderly patterns and others arranged randomly. Some numbers should be repeated. Show cards. *How many spots are there? Which did you find hardest to count?*
- Clap in a regular rhythm. *Count how many times I clap.* Children count out loud as you clap. *Now count to yourself as I clap.* Repeat, using irregular rhythms and/or different sounds.
- Arrange a group of children in a circle. Count around the circle. *How many of you are there?* Now the children swap places. *How many now?* Invite more children to join the circle. *If we count around the circle starting with Jack, who will say 4?*

- Ask children to make lollystick pictures.

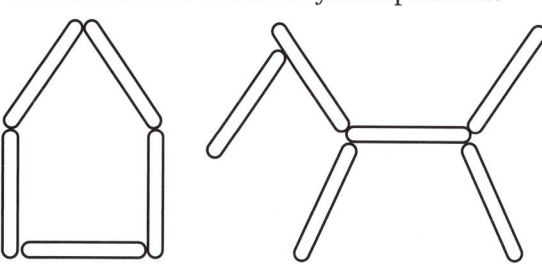

How many sticks did you use? Did anyone else use the same number? Who used 5 sticks? See if you can make a picture using 7 sticks.

Number rhymes

- Use rhymes to practise saying numbers in order, e.g. '1, 2, 3, 4, 5, once I caught a fish alive …'
- Ask children to count out objects/show number cards to match numbers in rhymes.

Counting in 2s

- Use number rhymes to practise counting in 2s, e.g. *Now in came the animals 2 by 2 …*
- Arrange children in a circle giving each child a number, starting from zero. Children pass a parcel around the circle, saying their numbers out loud. Play again, but this time miss out every other child (i.e. saying 0, 2, 4, 6, …). *Will number 10 get the parcel?*
- Use number cards attached to a blank number track. When counting together in 2s, remove numbers that are not said out loud to show a pattern of 2s.
- Line children in pairs and together count them in 2s. Check the total by together counting in 1s. Count again in 2s, emphasising that it helps us to find the total more quickly.
- Children count various objects, by arranging them in pairs to speed up the counting.
- Invite some children to stand in a line. Point to each child in turn. As you do so, they raise both hands and keep them in the air. Each time ask children to say the total number of hands raised.
- Children take a handful of objects and arrange them in 2s, returning any 'left over' items. They count their objects in 2s before checking with a partner.

- Use items that come in pairs (shoes, socks, gloves, ...) to practise counting in 2s, e.g. Hang different coloured pairs of socks on a line and count aloud. Remove/add some and count again.

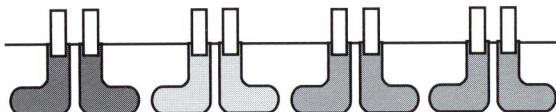

Counting in 10s
- Invite some children to stand in a line. As you point to each child in turn, they raise their fingers and keep them in the air. Children count aloud 10, 20, 30, 40, ... in time with the raising of the fingers.
- Use a 100 square to support counting together in 10s. Count up from zero to 100 and back again. Then use it to start counting on or back in 10s from any given multiple of 10.
- Children count in 10s up to 100 around a circle. Repeat several times with different starting children. Ask questions such as: *Who will be number 40 this time?*
- Give pairs of children a large number of items. Ask them to group their items in 10s and count in 10s to see how many they have. Emphasise how grouping in 10s speeds up counting.

Comparing numbers
- Give each child a tower built with 3, 4 or 5 interlocking cubes of one colour (e.g. red). Give them some loose cubes of a different colour (e.g. blue) and ask them to build a tower with the same number of cubes. *Now take your towers apart and match each red cube with a blue cube. Do you have 1 red cube for each blue cube? Have you got the same number of blue and red cubes?* Children may need to count to check.
- Use situations where you can match one quantity with another. *Are there enough plates for everyone ... pegs for our coats ... crayons for 1 each?*
- *I've got 3 oranges in this bag. Who can put the same number of oranges in my other bag?* Compare the sets of oranges.

- Compare non-matching sets:

Are there more apples or grapes?
- Invite 2 children to take a few counting objects each and lay them out. *Do you think Clare has more than John or fewer? How can we check?* Encourage counting and direct comparison by lining up or pairing off.
- Give children a collection of buttons and ask them to sort them into different types (round, shiny, wooden,...). *Which group has the most/least buttons in it? Are there more square buttons than round ones?*
- Take a handful of counting objects. Invite children to take their own handfuls in turn, giving instructions such as: *See if you can take more than me, see if you can take fewer than Sarah* ... Each time, check by counting and by direct comparison.
- Play 'More or less' with counting objects. Organise children in pairs and give each child a number card. They read their number and count out the appropriate number of counting objects. They compare their group with their partner's to see who has the greatest number.
- Play 'More or less' with numerals. Give each child a number card. They read their number to a partner and compare to see whose is the greatest number. They check with counting objects or on a number track.

Ordering quantities and numbers
- Describe and put groups of objects in order according to quantity, without counting, e.g. *lots of buttons, a few buttons, 1 button.*
- Ask 3 children to take some cubes each and build a tower. *Which is the tallest? Which is the shortest? Which is the middle sized tower?* Place the towers in order.
- Place 4 towers in order according to their heights, well spread out. Count how many cubes are in each tower and label them using

number cards. This will start to build a number track. Complete the number track by counting together from 1 asking children to insert appropriate number cards. Build the missing towers to check that the numbers are getting larger each time.

- Hang number cards in order on a washing line. Count along the washing line several times. Then ask children to close their eyes while you swap 2 of the numbers. *Open your eyes. Can you see what's wrong? Can you put them back in the right order?*

- Use number cards in order on a washing line. Turn some of the numbers so that they can't be seen. Point to 1 of the visible numbers and ask: *What number is this? Which number comes next?* Turn it over to check. Point to other visible numbers, asking questions such as: *What number comes after 5?... before 2? ... between 3 and 6?*

- Show 2 number cards with a space between them to represent a 'missing' number (so there is only 1 whole number answer). *What number comes between these 2?* Invite a child to find the card with the missing number. Repeat with other numbers, perhaps extending to problems with more than 1 possible answer.

Estimating

- Ask questions about quantities, offering 2 possible numbers as answers. Reinforce the idea that an estimate is a 'sensible guess'.

- Show a small box of toys. *Are there about 6 toys in here or about 40 toys?*

- *Are there about 20 children in class today or about 3?*

- Show a large collection of buttons. *Are there about 10 buttons in here or about 100?* You might need to count some of the buttons to get well beyond 10 to convince some children that it is not 10.

- Count out a few beads from a tub. *Who thinks they can take out about the same number of beads without counting? How close were you?*

- Repeat the above activity several times with 10 in 'your' group to develop estimation in terms of 'more than 10', 'less than 10', 'about 10'.

- *Take a handful of cubes. How many do you think you have picked up?* Ask children to count

them to find out. *Now take another handful of cubes, with your other hand. About how many do you think you will get this time?*

Using ordinal numbers

- Read a rhyme that contains ordinal numbers and actions. Repeat it several times, with children doing the actions. Use the rhyme to talk about order, e.g. *What did you do first?*

- Ask some children to form a line. Ask questions about their positions, e.g. *Who is last? Where is Ali in the line?*

- Give children instructions to make a line of coloured cubes, e.g. *Put the red cube first ... the blue cube after the third cube ...* Ask questions such as: *What position is the blue cube in?*

- Hang a selection of 1–10 number cards on a washing line in a muddled order. Ask children to read the numbers. *The numbers are muddled and need to be put in order. Which number comes first? Which number is last? Which number will be second?*

Introduction to Counting, reading and writing numbers: blocks CR10–13

General overview of the topic

Counting is at the heart of children's understanding of numbers and their ability to calculate. Block 10 develops children's counting and recognition of numbers beyond 10. Block 11 encourages children to estimate numbers of objects, and to use appropriate vocabulary to explain their reasoning. Block 12 focuses on counting in 10s and block 13 on counting in 2s.

Counting, reading and writing numbers 10: Development of number and counting skills
Children begin to read number names including zero. They count forwards and backwards to and from 100 and count back a given number using fingers to help. They recognise numerals to 100 and begin to write them. They develop reliable ways of counting objects by considering strategies for avoiding errors.

Counting, reading and writing numbers 11: Estimating numbers
Children begin to understand and use the language of estimation. They estimate small quantities and check by counting.

Real situations, e.g. deciding whether there are enough objects for a given purpose, are introduced so that children can begin to recognise where estimating can be useful.

They predict the positions of numbers on a partially labelled 1–10 number track, explaining their reasoning.

Counting, reading and writing numbers 12: Counting in 10s
Children learn to count in 10s from 10 to 100 and back again, and then from and to any multiple of 10 to 100.

Counting, reading and writing numbers 13: Saying every other number
Children count in 1s saying aloud only every other number. The resulting patterns are used to introduce the vocabulary 'odd' and 'even'. Children count in 2s, joining in and making up rhymes based on this. They count pairs of objects and explore how arranging objects in 2s can make counting easier.

Before they start, children need to

- count reliably up to 10 objects
- recognise small numbers of objects without counting
- recite the number names in order … continuing the count from a given number
- recite the number names in order, counting back from a given number
- begin to recognise and use numerals from 0 to 100

Concepts covered next year include

- counting on or back a given number of 10s, from a multiple of 10
- counting in steps of 5 from zero to 20 or more, then back again
- beginning to count on in steps of 3 from zero
- giving a sensible estimate of up to 30 objects

Chief misconceptions

- not matching the recitation of number names to objects when counting, e.g. saying the numbers correctly but pointing to each object at a different rate
- missing out an object or counting it twice when counting a set of objects
- pointing to a space between objects and assigning a number name to the space
- when counting in 1s, thinking that the number after 14 is 'fiveteen'
- when counting in 10s, thinking that the number after 90 is 'tenty'
- muddling 'teens' names with 'tens' names, such as 13 and 30
- thinking that an estimate should match the exact amount

Counting, reading and writing numbers 10.1 Numbers and words

Objectives • begin to read the first few number names, including zero
• recite the sequence: one, two, three ... to 100

Key idea	Numbers can be written as words.

Key words   zero, one, two ... ten, count

You need	1–6 dice
AS 1	washing line and numeral/number name cards with 0–10 and number name on reverse (AS 40–42) number name cards (AS 40, 42) large copy of any number rhyme collection of rhymes with number names (including teens numbers) number names on small pieces of paper

Introduction: oral work and mental calculation

Play 'Lucky number': Each child chooses a number 1–6 and writes this on a piece of paper. Choose children to come and roll the dice and say the number it lands on. Children who chose that number mark a tick on their paper. After 10 throws ask children to count up how many ticks they have for their number. Record totals on the board where all children can see them.
Which number came up most? Which number scored more than 4 ticks? Which numbers scored more than number 3? ...

Main teaching input and pupil activities

Direct teaching

1. *How many number names do you think we know?* Recite numbers together from 1 to 29. *Who can tell me the next number?* (30) *So we know at least 30.*

2. Share the key idea with children. Hang the numeral/number name cards on the washing line so that the numerals are facing the children. Invite a child to turn over the card showing number '10'. *What do you think is written on this card?* (word for the number 10) *Sometimes we call this the number name.* Ask all children to read the number name 'ten'. Repeat for other numbers asking children to predict the initial letter sound.

3. Turn cards back so that the numerals are facing the class. Show children name cards and ask them to match the words to the numerals. Check against the name on the back of the numeral cards. Begin with the easier words of ten and six, then move on to those that are harder to distinguish. *What can help us read some of the number names?* Discuss which sounds in the words help to identify the word, e.g. 'v' sound in five. *Which number names have 3 letters? Which number names start with 'f'? Which number name has the most letters?*

4. Place the cards in random order. Ask children to read the names as a whole class and then challenge individuals to read some.

5. Look at a number rhyme together, e.g. 'Hippety hop' from *Seven Dizzy Dragons*, Cambridge University Press 1997. Ask children to spot and read the number names.

6. *Let's see how many number names we can say.* Recite from 1 together, stopping after each '9' number to check that children know the name of the next multiple of 10.

Pupil activities

SUPPORT ★   Adult-supported

Read through the number names again in order and then in random order. Discuss ways of remembering number names, e.g. look for the 'v' in five so that five is not confused with four. Add the cards from the washing line and play a pairs matching game with numerals and number names.

CORE   Independent   AS 1

Children match numerals to number words.

EXTENSION   Adult-led

Share a collection of printed number rhymes (some including numbers between 10 and 20). Ask children to spot any number names. Record them and ask if anyone thinks they can write the matching numeral. Highlight the 'teen' pattern: Show children number names 'six' and 'sixteen'. *What do you notice about these 2 words?* (they both start with 'six'). *Which other numbers does this happen with?* Give children the opportunity to explore which other numbers this works for. Focus on how 'fifteen' is not 'fiveteen'.

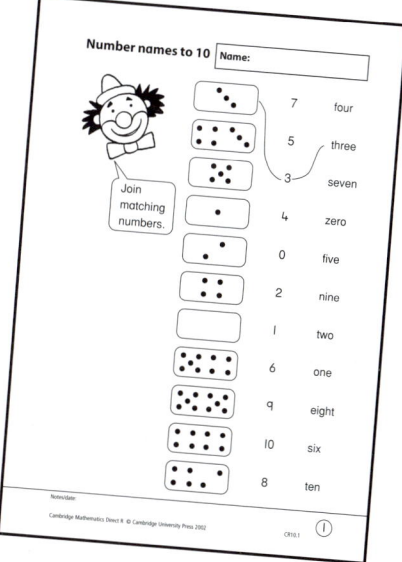

Plenary

Key idea: Numbers can be written as words.

1. Have number names on small pieces of paper around the classroom. *Can you find a number name?* When children have found one ask them to return to the carpet and try to read the word.

2. When all children have returned ask those children with 'six' to come and stand at front and show their word to remainder of class. Check to see they are all the same. Correct any errors, e.g. a child with 'seven' as it has the same first sound as 'six'. Repeat.

Family activity

- Be a number word detective. Look at home, in the street and other places to see where you can see the number names written.

Related play activities

- Give children opportunities to write number names on lists/labels ...
- Make a badge to say 'I am four/five'.

Counting, reading and writing numbers 10.2 Saying the next number

Objectives
- recognise and use numerals to beyond 10
- say the number name that comes after a given number name
- count reliably in other contexts

Key idea | We say the next number name when we count forwards.

Key words   count, ten, twenty, thirty ... one hundred

You need
   IP 2   IP 4   AS 2

1–10 number cards (1 per child for half the class) (AS 41)
cards with number names one to ten (1 per child for half the class) (AS 42)
puppet
counting stick
equipment for physical counting activities
empty number track (AS 48)

Introduction: oral work and mental calculation

Choose 1 or 2 'number name' helpers (leave an even number of children). Give half of the rest of the class numeral cards 1–10. Give the other half number name cards one to ten.

On command 'go' children find their partner, e.g. 1 and one, and then sit down. Children who are unsure of what their number name says may go to the helper for help in reading number names. Repeat, swapping roles.

Main teaching input and pupil activities

Direct teaching

1. Share the key idea with the children. Show children the word 'count'. *If we see this word written down, what is it telling us to do?*
2. Look at IP 4. *The are lots of different numbers in the square. Who can come and point to a number and tell us what it is? Who can find the number 10?* ... Target children with appropriate numbers.
3. Choose a child. *Look at the square and choose a number. Keep it secret, but clap/jump to show us what it is.* Ask the other children to count out loud. Check to see if the number reached is the number chosen.
4. Use a counting stick. Count to 10 together to set a rhythm. *Look at the picture. Who can show me the line of numbers we have just counted?* Count to 10 again pointing at the numbers in the square. Then using the stick alone start at 21 and count to 30. *Look at the picture. Who can show me the line of numbers we have just counted?* Ask a child to point to the numerals as you all count again.
5. Repeat for different decades beginning with 31, 51, 81, ... Make sure children know the name of the next multiple of 10 each time. *Let's try and count all the way to 100.*
6. *Which number comes after 5?* (6 because when we count we say 5, 6, ...) *What number comes after 16?* Repeat increasing the value of the numbers.

Pupil activities

SUPPORT ★   Adult-supported   IP 2
Use a puppet:
Practise saying the next number, e.g. puppet says 2, 3, 4, 5; children say 6. Repeat within same decade, bridge across 10, then up to 20. Move beyond 20 if confident.

Let the puppet make counting mistakes and children correct them, e.g. 3, 4, 6, 7, 8; 8, 9, 10, 12, 11, 13; nine, ten, eleven, twelve, threeteen, fourteen, ...thirteen, fourteen, fiveteen, sixteen. Use IP 2 to practise counting objects. Ask a child to cross out each one as the rest count slowly.

CORE   Adult-led

Use an empty number track: Point to each square as you count along stopping to let children say the next number, e.g. 11, __, 13, 14, __, 16, 17, __, 19, __. Repeat with sequences that bridge a tens number. Ask children as a whole group and also as individuals.

Children work in pairs to try different activities, e.g. hopping, throwing a bean bag into a bucket, ... counting how many their partner can do of each activity. Record by drawing pictures of the activity and writing the number.

EXTENSION   Independent   AS 2, IP 4

Fill in the missing numbers, using IP 4 for support.

Plenary

Key idea: We say the next number name when we count forwards.

1. Use the puppet to say a number. Ask children to say together what number comes next. Repeat several times then target individual children with appropriate numbers.

2. Increase the challenge by asking 3 children to continue the count.

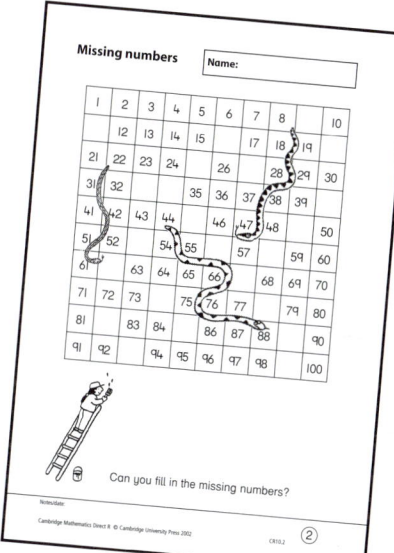

Family activity

- Practise reciting number names to 100.

Related play activities

- Look at the pattern in page numbers in books. Can you find a book with more than 50 pages?
- Count how many hops a friend can do without stopping or how many steps from one end of the play area to the other.

Counting, reading and writing numbers 10.3 Count down

Objectives
- recite the number names in order, counting back from a given number
- start at a given number name and stop at another when counting back
- count back several numbers from a given number name using fingers to help
- say the number name that comes before a given number name

Key idea | Counting back from 67 to 62 is like counting back from 7 to 2.

Key words   count back (from to), ten, twenty ... one hundred, puzzle

You need   washing line and number cards to 20 and beyond
a selection of counting back number rhymes
puppet
a box/container and counters for each pair for Core
0–100 number track (AS 46, 47), 1–6 dice and number cards 50–100 for
Extension

Introduction: oral work and mental calculation

Place one number on the washing line, e.g. 8, and give out about 4 other cards to pairs of children, e.g. 3, 4, 6 and 9. Ask pairs to come and place their number card on the line where they think it goes. Ask other children to show 'thumbs up' if they would have put it in the same place or 'thumbs down' if not. Ask one child to explain their view. When all the cards are on the washing line in the correct place ask children to say the sequence of numbers including missing ones. Count forwards and back. Repeat with other number cards.

Main teaching input and pupil activities

Direct teaching

1. Share and act out some number rhymes that use counting back from 10, e.g. 'Five currant buns in a baker's shop', 'Ten green bottles' or 'Ten little teddies'/'Seven dizzy dragons'/ 'Rockets' *from Seven Dizzy Dragons*, Cambridge University Press 1997.

2. Practise counting back quickly, e.g. from 5/7/10 to zero, from 5 to 3, from 8 to 1, from 9 to 4. You could make it into a game like 'Simon says' with children sitting out if they go beyond the number. Repeat, asking children to count back a number up to 5 from a larger number. Remind them how to use their fingers to keep track.

3. Use a boastful puppet to demonstrate some 'clever' counting back: *You can count back from*

5 to 3 but I can count back from 25 to 23. Let children try. It may help to whisper the 20 and say the digit louder in each number. *I can count back from 55 to 53. Can you? ...* Do plenty of examples without bridging multiples of 10.

4. *My puppet is not very good at the 'tricky' numbers that come next to 20, 30, 40, 50, ... Can you help him by counting forward and then back. Change direction when I clap.* Say together: 26, 27, 28, 29, 30 (clap), 29, 28, 27, 26. *What number was next to 30?* Repeat up to and back from other multiples of 10.

5. *Let's try counting back all the way to zero from 50. Be careful at the tricky numbers.* Ask groups and individuals to count back from, e.g. 31 to 25, 68 to 63, 99 to 92, 73 to 68, 14 to 8, 25 to 18. Repeat asking children to count back a number up to 5 from a larger number. Remind them how to use their fingers to keep track.

6. *Here are some puzzles: How do you know what number name comes before 45, 82, 50, 70, 100 ...* Ask children to explain. Encourage them to use 'count back'.

7. Introduce the core activity to the whole class. Ask 2 able children to demonstrate counting the number of counters on the table. Make sure they start and end with 'zero' for none on the table.

Pupil activities

SUPPORT ★   Adult-led
Practise the rhymes and counting back from 10 as in Direct teaching 1 and 2.

CORE   Independent
Children work in pairs. They pick up several handfuls of counters to count and put them in a box. One child counts forwards as they take the counters out of the box one by one. The other child counts backwards as they put them one by one into the box. They should reach zero on the table as the last one goes into the box.

EXTENSION   Adult-supported
Play 'Count back': Use a 0–100 number track, a 1–6 dice and a set of number cards 50–100. Children take turns to take a number card and place their counter on that number on the square. They throw the dice and, using their fingers to keep track, count back the number shown. They then check, with the rest of the group watching for mistakes, by counting the squares as they move their counter back. If correct they receive a counter. The child with most counters wins.

Plenary
Key idea: Counting back from 67 to 62 is like counting back from 7 to 2.

1. Ask children from the support group to recite a rhyme.

2. Do the core activity together as a class with you moving the counters as children count.

3. Say a sequence of numbers going backwards but miss one out. *What's the missing number?* Repeat but with children saying own sequences and missing a number out for others to identify.

Family activity
- Practise counting backwards from any number up to 100.

Related play activity
- Use a book with obvious page numbers. One child opens the book, says the page number and asks another other child to say the number on the page before.

Counting, reading and writing numbers 10.4 Number games

Objectives
- recite the number names in order to 100, continuing the count from a given number
- begin to write numerals correctly

Key idea | We can use numbers to make games.

Key words count on, count back, pattern, bigger than, smaller than, right (correct)

You need A3 version of AS 3

 AS 3

selection of board games with numbers

dice, a marker or playing piece for all

sets of small objects (of about 50 for each Support pair
  and 100 for each core pair)

Introduction: oral work and mental calculation

Invite 2 children to choose a number each between 1 and 100. Limit the range as appropriate. Record the numbers so all children can see. *Which is the larger/smaller number?* Invite another child to toss a coin. If the coin lands on heads count forwards from the smaller to larger number and if the coin lands on tails count backwards from the larger to smaller number.

Main teaching input and pupil activities

Direct teaching

1. Look at a selection of board games with numbers. Discuss the games. *Why do they have numbers? Which is the greatest/smallest number? Are the numbers in a pattern? Does every space have a number on? Are the same numbers used on all the games?*

2. *We are going to make a game with numbers.* Model the game 'Count from 10' on an A3 copy of AS 3 with the children. Write the name of the game in the middle. *Our game is going to have some special squares, some are going to be 'miss a turn' and some 'have 2 turns'.* Invite children to come and choose where the squares will be. Use 2 different coloured pens to colour these squares (3 of each).

3. *Some of the squares are going to be for counting forwards. We need to write a number bigger than 10 on 13 of the squares.* Invite children to select numbers and write them in any space they choose. *If you land on one of these squares you must count out loud forwards from 10 to that number.*

4. *The other squares are going to be for counting backwards so we need to choose numbers that are smaller than 10.* Invite children to come and fill in remaining squares. *If you land on 1 of these squares you count back from 30 to that number. If you get the counting right, then you win a counter. The winner of the game will be the person with the most counters. You can choose which square to put your marker on, then you take turns to throw the dice and move round the board the way the arrows are pointing.*

5. Divide the class into 2 groups and each have 3 turns of the game.

Pupil activities

SUPPORT ★ Adult-supported AS 3

Help pairs of children to make a game board for 'Who has the most?': *We are going to use the numbers 1 to 10.* Children write numbers randomly on the squares on AS 3.

Give each pair a selection of small objects (no more than 50) to place in the middle of their board.

Children choose where to put their markers, then take it in turns to roll the dice and move that number of spaces. They read the number on the square they have landed on and count out that number of objects from the middle. When all the objects in the middle have been taken each player counts to see how many they have. The player with the most is the winner.

CORE Adult-led AS 3

Each pair makes a game similar to the support activity, using numbers 1 to 20. They will need a set of about 100 small objects. Also include 'miss a turn' and '2 turns' squares.

EXTENSION Independent AS 3

Children make their own 'Count from' game as modelled in the main teaching. They may choose any multiple of 10 as long as they are able to write larger and smaller numerals. They find a friend to play it with.

Plenary

Key idea: We can use numbers to make games.

1. Use one of the games made by the extension group to give further practice in counting.
2. Look for problems writing numerals and discuss these.
3. Discuss the games. *Which game was good? Why? What do you think is the best part of your game? How could you make it better?*

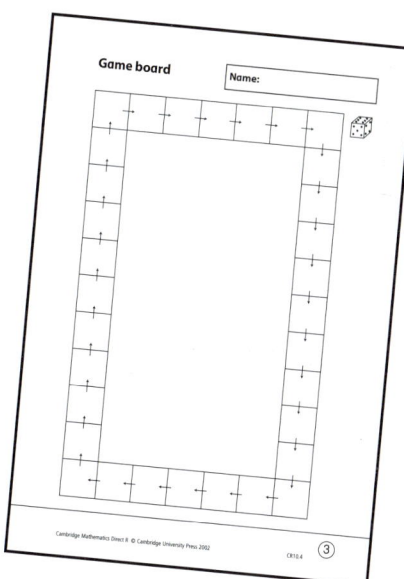

Family activity

- Children take home the game they made in the lesson and play with others at home. Alternatively ask children to make their own game at home and bring into school.

Related play activity

- Play board games involving numbers and counting.

Counting, reading and writing numbers 10.5 Counting without mistakes

Objectives
- count collections of objects in different arrangements
- recognise counting errors
- count reliably a set of everyday objects and count collections, etc.

Key idea | We can use different ways to help us count.

Key words   count on, count back

You need   3 sets of 0–10 number cards (AS 40, 41)

[IP 5] [AS 4]

0–10 number name cards

puppet

objects for counting, e.g. plastic teddies, cubes, pieces of construction kit

pots containing 10–20 objects

pictures with more then 10 objects to count

sets of 1–20 number cards for Extension (AS 41, 43)

Introduction: oral work and mental calculation

1. Read through number name cards. Repeat but with cards in random order. Give each child a card with a numeral 0–10 on and ask children to show their numeral card when that number name card is shown.

2. Play 'Pairs': Put all numeral cards and number name cards face down. Invite children in turn to turn over a numeral card and a number name card and see if they match.

Main teaching input and pupil activities

Direct teaching

1. *We are going to think about the best ways to count objects without making any mistakes.* Use a puppet to count several groups of objects, some with errors. Ask children to show thumbs up if the puppet is right and thumbs down for a mistake. *Tell me what went wrong,* e.g. saying 2 numbers for 1 object, touching an object and not saying a number, counting an object twice.

2. *Let's give the puppet some help. What things must he remember so that he will not make any mistakes?* Elicit: say 1 number name for each object, arrange objects so that they will not be counted twice, where objects cannot be touched/moved remember his starting point.

3. Make a circle with a set of objects. *Where shall we start counting? How can you remember?* Discuss strategies.

4. Change the arrangement to a rectangular array (in rows and columns). *Who can show me how to count these objects carefully? Has anyone got a different way?*

5. Use various groups of balloons on IP 5 to give children practice in counting sets of objects where they cannot touch them. Show children how they can 'point to them in the air' to help them keep track of which ones they have counted.

Pupil activities

SUPPORT ★   Independent   AS 4
Children practise counting sets of objects arranged in different ways.

CORE   Adult-led
Give pairs of children pots containing between 10 and 20 objects to tip out onto table or carpet. *Would it be very easy to count the objects as they are now? Can you arrange them so that it would be easier to count them?* Discuss the different

arrangements and ask children to count them. Pairs show how they counted their set of objects. Put the objects back in the pots and swap them. Challenge children to arrange their new set in a different way.

EXTENSION   Adult-supported

Develop Direct teaching **5.** using IP 5 or other pictures. Give children opportunities to explain orally how they would count objects, e.g. I would count across, I would count down. Discuss how different arrangements suit different ways. Show children an arrangement of up to 20 objects and ask them to count how many without touching, then show their answer using number cards. Repeat for other groups of objects.

Plenary

Key idea: We can use different ways to help us count.

1. Use the puppet to count groups of objects, making the occasional error for children to correct. Ask children for help or to give suggestions as to what to do next in some examples.

2. Ask children from each group to explain what they had to do. Elicit the main things to remember to do when counting: say 1 number name for each object, arrange objects so that they will not be counted twice, where objects cannot be touched/moved remember the starting point.

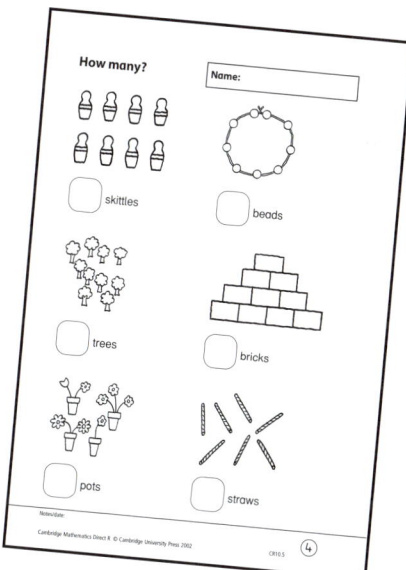

Family activity

● Find different things that can be counted and then count to see how many there are, e.g. all the shoes, books on a shelf, teddies, pieces of a puzzle.

Related play activities

● Count items in the play house.
● Check that all the pieces in a jigsaw puzzle are there by counting pieces and matching to the number on the box.

Counting, reading and writing numbers 11.1 Guess the number

Objectives
- guess the number of items and check by counting
- recite the number sequence: *one, two, three ... ,* overcoming difficulties and recognising recitation errors
- **SP** make simple estimates and predictions

Key idea | We can guess how many we have before we count.

Key words   guess, how many? more/less than, about, between, nearly

You need   socks, cubes

washing line and large 1–20 number cards (AS 41, 43)
objects for guessing how many
small whiteboards (or pieces of paper)
clear containers containing objects to be guessed

Introduction: oral work and mental calculation

Divide class into groups of about 4 and give each group a sock containing between 10 and 20 cubes. *Feel the sock and count how many cubes are in the sock. Write down the number of cubes you think is in your sock.* Swap socks and repeat. Ask children to compare answers with the group they swapped with. Empty out the cubes and count to check.

Main teaching input and pupil activities

Direct teaching

1. *We can guess how many we have before we count. To make a good guess we need to think about the number of things that we have to guess, but not actually count to find out how many.*

2. *Close you eyes and imagine what 5 pencils look like.* Show children 3 pencils briefly. *Were there more than 5?* Come to an agreement that there were not. *We say we guess there were fewer (less) than 5.* Count the pencils. *We guessed the number of pencils was less than 5, so we made a good guess.* Discuss numbers that would have been a good guess. *What about 30?* (no, because 30 is a lot more than 3 but 5 is only a little bit more than 3)

3. Repeat with different groups of objects. Introduce vocabulary through questioning, e.g. *Are there more than 3, about 5, nearly 10: is the number more than 10? Is it less than 20? Is it between 10 and 20?*

4. Use IP 11 to give children practice in guessing how many objects in a picture. Before showing the picture to the children cover over some parts. Reveal each part briefly. Ask children to share guesses and then look and count to establish which was a good guess.

Pupil activities

SUPPORT ★   Adult-supported

Show children groups of between 1 and 10 different objects. Ask them to 'guess how many' and record their guess. *Are there more than 3, about 5, nearly 10 ... ?* Decide on the best method to use to count objects and invite 1 child to come and count how many there are. Decide which were 'good' guesses.

CORE   Adult-led

Children guess how many there are in randomly arranged groups of up to 20 objects. Cover the objects with a cloth. Remove cloth briefly and then cover again. Ask children to record their guess. Invite 1 child to come and check how many by counting. Decide which were 'good' guesses. Extend to showing children collections of objects where not all can be seen, e.g. buttons in a jar. *Why is it harder to guess now?*

EXTENSION   Independent

Children work in pairs. Child A briefly shows a group of objects to child B and then hides them. Child B records their guess and then checks how many by counting. Both children decide if it was a 'good guess' or not. A selection of items in clear containers that can be seen but not easily counted could be available for this group to work with. Extend the number of objects to be estimated to about 30.

Plenary

Key idea: We can guess how many we have before we count.

1. Invite a pair of children from the extension group to show 1 of the jars and ask them to explain what they had to do. *What was your guess?* Did anyone make a different guess. Involve other children by asking them to show thumbs up if they think it is a good guess and thumbs down if not. Identify how many were in the jar and establish what was a good guess.

2. Reinforce that a good guess is not just the right answer but a number that is close: it can be more or less than the actual number.

Family activity

● Make a 'guess how many' game at home. Fill a see-through container with some objects and ask people at home to guess how many they think are in the container without counting. Open the container and count how many to see which people made a good guess.

Related play activity

● How many sweets in the jar? Have a clear container of sweets on display and a post box for children to post their guess in. At the end of the week count the sweets and see who made a good guess.

Counting, reading and writing numbers 11.2 Introducing estimating

Objectives
- begin to understand and use the language of estimation in practical contexts
- check an estimate by counting
- overcome difficulties and recognise recitation errors
- **SP** make simple estimates and predictions

Key idea	We can estimate before we count.

Key words   count, estimate, how many?, nearly, more/less than, about, between

You need

IP 12

collections or pictures of objects to estimate
opaque container with lid, transparent container
books with fewer than 30 words on each page
marbles, pasta shapes, ...
socks containing 5, 20 and 35 cubes and washing line

Introduction: oral work and mental calculation

Count on round the circle. Ask children to stop when you clap. Ask questions involving counting on/back from the number you reached, e.g. *Natalie said 12. Who will say 14? Count on 3 more. Count back to 8. How many did we count back?...* Repeat, restarting the count at an appropriate number.

Main teaching input and pupil activities

Direct teaching

1. Introduce children to the word 'estimate'. *Estimate means the same as 'guess how many'.* Ask a child to estimate how many pencils in the pot. *When we estimate how many there are, we are saying how many we think there are and not counting the exact number. An estimate tells us 'about' how many.*

2. Explore the idea of a good estimate. *Sometimes our estimates are nearly right and are 'good' and useful estimates.* Discuss how to make a good estimate. (Thinking about how many there are, thinking about something similar that we know the number of, imagining what 5 or 10 of the object look like, ...)

3. Use IP 12 to give children practice in estimating the number of objects shown, e.g. the number of birds, squirrels, animals,

acorns ... Guide them in the first few examples into thinking about their estimate in relation to a given number, saying whether it is more or less than a number rather than estimating an exact amount. Ask children to answer by saying *My estimate is ...* After children have given estimates, count to find out how many there are. Reinforce that an estimate is not necessarily the exact number but may be close to the exact number.

4. Put 10 pasta shapes into an opaque container. Ask children to listen to what 10 shapes sound like as you shake it. Tip them out and secretly put about 20 shapes in. Shake again for children to estimate the number. Ask them to record their estimate to encourage independent thought. Discuss the estimates and count the shapes.

Pupil activities

SUPPORT ★ Adult-led

Place 4 marbles in an opaque container. Shake the container. *Let's estimate how many marbles there are. Do you think it is less than 20? Less than 10? Less than 5?* Encourage children to answer using 'estimate'. Empty the container and count. Repeat with a larger number of marbles, e.g. 20. Shake it. *Does it sound like there are more marbles? Will our estimates be larger or smaller numbers? ... more than 5 ... 10 ... 20 ... 100?* Ask children to estimate then count. Repeat with marbles in a transparent container.

CORE   Independent

Children estimate the number of words on a page in a book and then check by counting. Ask children to record their estimates using a coloured pencil or felt-pen. Repeat for different pages.

EXTENSION   Adult-supported

Explore the statement 'All pages in these books have the same number of words'. Ask children to give their views and then to find evidence by making their own estimates of how many words on each page and checking by counting. Estimate which page in a book has most words. Discuss with children how they will check to see if their estimate is correct. *Do you need to count the words on every page?*

Plenary

Key idea: We can estimate before we count.

1. Make an 'Estimation washing line': Peg 1 sock in the middle of the washing line. Ask children to come and feel the sock briefly and then estimate if the next sock has more or fewer cubes. Encourage them to feel the second sock, come to a consensus. Choose a child to hang it in an appropriate place. Repeat for the third sock. When all socks are ordered on the washing line, tell the children which sock has 20 cubes and ask them to estimate how many are in the others. Record some of the estimates and check them by counting.

2. Ask children from the extension group to explain how they made their estimates and what they found.

Family activity

● Estimate how many words are on the page of your reading book. Can you estimate which pages have more words and which pages have fewer words?

Related play activity

● Children match labels 'more than 10', 'less than 20', 'between 10 and 20' to containers of objects and then count to see if it was a good estimate.

Counting, reading and writing numbers 11.3 Too many or too few?

Objectives
- begin to understand and use the language of estimation in practical contexts involving having enough
- count objects arranged randomly by counting systematically without touching them
- **SP** make simple estimates and predictions

Key idea	We can estimate to see if we have enough.

Key words count, how many? estimate, just under, just over, too many, too few, enough, not enough

You need	hoops and 0–30 number cards (AS 40, 41, 43, 44) box of sweets or similar groups of items for Support group to estimate in the play house sets of objects to estimate

Introduction: oral work and mental calculation

Give each child a number card: choose numbers that are appropriate to the level of individual children but not too wide a range. Place a number of hoops on the floor. *Stand in a hoop if you have a number that ... is bigger than 10, ... is less than 8, ... is more than 15, ... is between 20 and 30, ...*

Main teaching input and pupil activities

Direct teaching

1. Share the key idea with children. *I've got a handful of pencils here.* Ask 8 children to stand up. *Are there enough pencils for each child to have 1? How can we find out?* Give 1 pencil to each child. *Does everyone have a pencil?* (No) *We say there are not enough pencils for everyone.*

2. Repeat with other examples where there are either too few or too many objects to match a group of children. Begin using smaller numbers of objects and extend to numbers relating to the whole class, e.g. *Are there enough sheets of paper for everyone to have 1? Are there enough sweets in the packet for everyone to have 1?* Encourage children to use some of the key words in expressing their ideas, e.g. 'I think there are not enough sweets', 'I think there are too few sweets for everyone to have 1' ...

Pupil activities

SUPPORT ★   Independent

Set a scenario in a play house where some items have been removed or added so that there is not exactly 6 of everything. Ask children to investigate whether each of 6 people could have one of everything. Find out which items there are not enough of and which items are there too many of. Ask children to be ready to show what they have found out in the plenary. They record in their own way, e.g. lists with pictures and marks or numbers to show how many more or less are needed.

CORE   Adult-supported

Have a selection of objects in sets of different numbers. Investigate if there are enough of each item for each person in the group to have 1. Ask children to estimate whether they think there will be enough for each time. Invite different children in the group to come and check out the group's estimates either by sharing objects out, or by counting the number of objects and comparing this number to the number of children in the group.

EXTENSION   Adult-led

Are there enough pencils for each person in the group to have 2? Children estimate. *How can we find out? How many do we need?* Invite children to find out how accurate their estimate was by sharing objects out. Show children larger sets of objects (exact multiples of the number of children). *Can you estimate how many pencils you will each have if I share all these between you?* Invite a child to share out objects and see how many they each get and compare this number to their estimates. Discuss why estimates may differ.

Plenary

Key idea: We can estimate to see if we have enough.

1. Ask the support group to share their work. Ask children to show how they have recorded and to explain whether there were enough or not of each object. Encourage them to use the vocabulary of estimation. Invite children to bring items from the play house and show the rest of the class.

2. Ask questions based on numbers of groups within the class, e.g. *Are there enough girls in the class for each boy to have a partner?*

Family activity

● Help set the table at home and see if there are enough of each item.

Related play activity

● In the play house see if there are enough cups and saucers, plates, knives, forks, ... for each child to have 1.

Counting, reading and writing numbers 11.4 Finding positions on a number track 1

Objective
- point to different places on a number track with only 1 and 10 marked and say what number would be in that position
- **SP** make simple estimates and predictions

Key idea We can estimate where numbers go on a number track to 10.

Key words before, after, next, between, right (correct), middle

You need

| IP 3 | AS 5 | AS 6 |

washing line and number cards
blank floor 1–10 number track
empty number tracks for Core (AS 48)

Introduction: oral work and mental calculation

Place a sequence of small numbers in random order on a washing line. Invite children to swap 2 numbers till all the numbers are in the correct order. Repeat for different sequences. Challenge children to sort the 'washing' in a given number of turns.

Main teaching input and pupil activities

Direct teaching

1. Use IP 3. Write in numbers 1 and 10 at either end of the empty number track at the bottom. *What number does my number track start with? What number does it end at? Some of the numbers are missing. What other numbers do you think might belong on this number track?* Establish that numbers between 1 and 10 will fill the spaces on the number track. Write in the numbers between 1 and 10. Point to different numbers and ask children what they are. Rub them out leaving 1 and 10. *Which numbers are in the middle of the track?* (5 and 6)

2. Point to the position for number 4 and ring it. *What number do you think this is?* Invite children to suggest answers. *You have estimated which numbers might go in this space.* Ask children if they can suggest a way to check which is the right number. Elicit counting on from 1. *Who can write in the numbers from 1?*

3. Rub out numbers other than 1 and 10 and repeat **2.** for the space for 6. Discuss how 4 is just before 5 and 6 is just after 5.

4. Point to space for 8. *What number belongs here?* Take estimates and reasons, e.g. the space is nearly at 10. *Can anyone think of a different way to check this space: it is nearly at 10.* Elicit counting back from 10.

5. Stress the key idea. Point to 3 stepping stones on the 0–20 track and ring them. Challenge children in the extension group to take the IP and work as a group to estimate what numbers go on the 3 stones. They should all record their estimates before checking by counting and writing in all the numbers to 20.

Pupil activities

SUPPORT ★ Adult-led

Use a blank floor track and fill in 1 and 10. Ask a child to stand on a space. *Which number do you think Ann is standing on?* Take estimates and check. *Where shall I start counting from?* Focus on counting on from 1 till children are secure with this, and then move to counting back from 10 where appropriate.

CORE Adult-supported AS 5

Reinforce the strategy of estimating from 10 for spaces near to 10 and from 5 or 6 for spaces near the middle. Use a blank number track to give further examples. Children complete AS 5, filling in only the spaces highlighted, first with their estimate in 1 colour and then with the number arrived at by counting in another colour. Circulate among the group, giving children the opportunity to explain which strategy they are using for the different numbers.

EXTENSION Independent IP3 AS 6

When children have completed their challenge from Direct teaching 5., they complete AS 6 by estimating the positions of the cloud numbers and writing them on the track in one colour. Check by counting whether the estimates match the correct positions of the numbers 11–20.

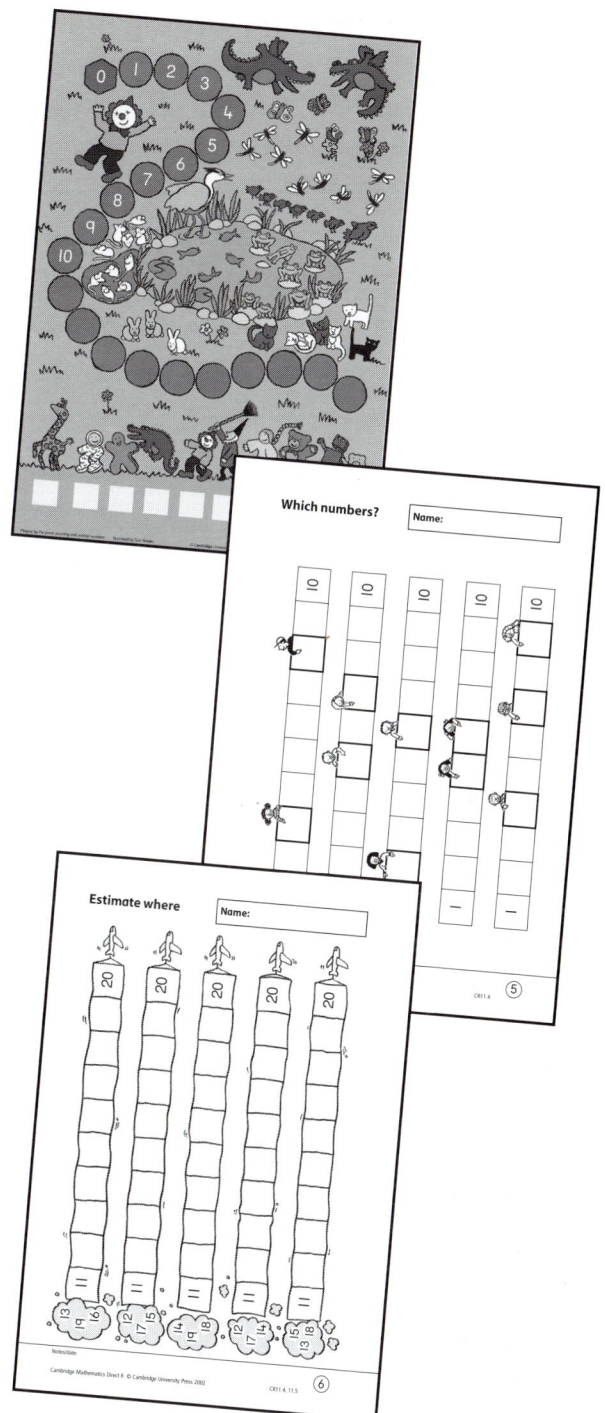

Plenary

Key idea: We can estimate where numbers go on a number track to 10.

1. Look at the results from the core group. *Did you put your estimates in the right positions?* Pick children to explain their thinking each time. Elicit that it is useful to know which side of the middle to place the number and whether it is near to one end of the track or the other. Also look at where you have put your other numbers.

2. Ask children from the extension group to share their work. *What are the end and the middle numbers this time? How did you know where to place the numbers on AS 6?*

Family activity

● Children take home an empty number track. Help them to choose 3 numbers to put on, e.g. their age, the number in their family, the age of the dog, …

Related play activities

● Have a counting stick marked with 1 and 10 and a pot with only 3 other 'sticky' numbers in. Children estimate the positions of the numbers by sticking them on.

● Make a line of house pictures and spaces for house numbers. Number the first and last house. Place house numbers in a pot. Children take out a number without looking and estimate its place. Check by counting.

Counting, reading and writing numbers 11.5 Finding positions on a number track 2

Objectives
- point to different places on a number track with only 1 and 10 marked and say what number would be in that position
- extend to using a number track beyond 10
- **SP** make simple estimates and predictions

Key idea	We can estimate where numbers go on a number track.

Key words   count, before, after, next, between

You need

IP 3	AS 6	AS 7

digit cards for all (AS 41)
empty number tracks (AS 48)
puppet
small sticky notes for numbers
1–12 number cards (AS 41, 43)

Introduction: oral work and mental calculation

Say the rhyme 'Here comes the bus':

Here comes the bus, it's going to stop.
Hurry up children, in you pop.
__ inside, and __ on the top.
How many altogether?

Children use digit cards to show how many are on the bus.

Main teaching input and pupil activities

Direct teaching

1. Use IP 3. Fill in number 20 on the last stepping-stone. *What number does my number track start with? What number does it end at? Some of the numbers are missing: what other numbers do you think might belong on this number track?* Establish that numbers from 11 to 20 will fill the spaces on the track and write them in.

2. Point to different numbers and ask individuals what they are. Let's hide the first 10 numbers. *What number does the track begin with now?* (11) *What numbers are in the middle?* (15, 16) Rub out the numbers leaving 11 and 20.

3. Show numbers 13, 18, 15 on sticky notes. *These numbers have fallen off the number track. Our puppet says he can put them back on.* Puppet places numbers in 3 spaces randomly. *Has he got it right?* Invite children to explain why the

puppet is wrong. Ask questions, e.g. *Which number should be in the middle? Which end is 13 near to? What comes between 15 and 20?* Ask individuals to place the numbers and then check by counting. Encourage children to count on from 10 to check number 13, on 2 from 13 to check 15 and back 2 from 20 to check 18.

4. Repeat activity. Give children opportunities to explain which strategy they are using to position numbers on the number track and encourage the use of key words.

Pupil activities

SUPPORT ★   Adult-supported   AS 7
Help children to complete AS 7. They could initially write the numbers in the cloud on small pieces of paper to estimate the positions of the numbers and then write in the numbers when they have checked by counting. Ask children to explain which method they are using and reinforce the correct use of key words vocabulary.

CORE   Independent   AS 6

Children complete AS 6 by estimating the positions of the cloud numbers and writing them on the track in one colour. Check by counting whether the estimates match the correct positions of the numbers 11–20. Write these in another colour.

EXTENSION   Adult-led   IP 3

Work as a group with the empty number track at the bottom of IP 3. Write in pairs of start and finish numbers, e.g. 6 and 15, 9 and 18, … Discuss the middle numbers each time, then give children 3 'sticky' numbers for children to position roughly. Check by counting. Dispense with the number track and write start and finish numbers some distance apart on the board. Repeat the activity. Try making the 'number track' longer than 10. Children can then work in pairs like this with 1 partner challenging the other.

Plenary

Key idea: We can estimate where numbers go on a number track.

1. Give 12 children number cards 1–12. Ask numbers 1 and 12 to stand at each end of an imaginary number track and show their cards. Ask the other children with cards to position themselves, beginning with 6, 3, 11, … Remind children to think about the spaces they need to leave for other children. Ask questions about positions as they move to highlight the key words.

2. Repeat perhaps with an even longer line. *Can you get your position about right first time so you don't have to move?*

Family activity

- Use ace to 10 from one suit of a pack of cards. Place ace (1) and 10 on the table with the 8 other cards face down between them to make a number track. Shuffle remaining cards and place face down. Take one card at a time and place on the number track until all the spaces are covered.

Related play activity

- Cover up some of the numbers in sequence displays around the class. Can children identify what numbers are missing?

Counting, reading and writing numbers 12.1 Counting in 10s

Objectives • count on in 10s from 10
• recite the sequence ten, twenty, thirty … one hundred forwards and backwards
• **SP** recognise and recreate simple patterns

Key idea | We can count in 10s.

Key words   ten, twenty, thirty, … one hundred, tens numbers, pattern

You need   lots of small items, e.g. paper clips, cubes, buttons
0–100 number track to cut up (AS 46, 47)

IP 4	IP 8	scissors and glue sticks

about 600 straws and 60 rubber bands

AS 8	AS 9	small see-through bags with sets of 10 objects

large number cards, 10, 20, … (AS 45)

Introduction: oral work and mental calculation

Give pairs a pot containing small items to count (choose an appropriate number up to 100 according to ability). One child counts forwards starting from zero (none on the table) and says the next number as they take each item out of the pot. The other child counts back as they put them back in, ending with zero if they have both counted correctly. Swap roles and remember the total number. Count along the number track together pointing to each number. Children put their hands up when you say their number.

Main teaching input and pupil activities

Direct teaching

1. Look at the number track. Ask children to count with you to 10 as you point to each number. Draw a ring round the numeral. *Let's count another 10 numbers: we can use our fingers to help us know when we have reached the tenth number.* When you reach 20, ring it. Repeat to 100. Say the numbers together again, saying the tens numbers loudly and the rest quietly.

2. Have IP 4 at hand. *Now we will say just the numbers with a ring.* Record them on the shirts on the washing line as children say 10, 20, 30, … 100. *These numbers are the tens numbers: we have counted in 10s starting at 10.*

3. Cut the number track into 10 sections after each multiple of 10. Hold up each section in order: *Where is the tens number?* (at the end) *Can you say it? Look at the first part of the number to help.* Stick the sections to the board to make a 100 square. Ask a child to point to the

tens numbers as you count together again. *We have made the number track into a square.* Compare it with the one on IP 4. *Can you see the tens numbers in this number square?* Talk about the patterns of counting numbers and zeros that make the tens pattern.

4. Look at IP 8. Focus children's attention on the hands at the bottom. *We have 10 fingers and that can help us to count in 10s.* Show children how to make a 'tens flash' by making a fist with both hands then opening both fists as 'ten' is said. Repeat counting to 100 in 10s from 10 using 'tens flash'.

5. Use the blank number track at the bottom of IP 8. Fill in the tens pattern numbers from 0 to 100. *Can you say the tens pattern? 0, 10, 20, 30, … 100* Ask a child to rub out one of the tens and say the count again. Repeat several times.

Pupil activities

SUPPORT ★   Independent   IP 8   AS 8
Children cut out the parts of the caterpillar's body (or have them pre-cut). Place and then stick

them in order to make a 'tens caterpillar' they can use IP 8 for matching the numbers. Children add feelers, legs and a tail to make it look realistic.

CORE   Adult-supported   AS 9

Have straws and rubber bands available. Ask children each to make a bundle of 10 straws. Count round a circle together in 10s: each child holds up their bundle in turn (and keeps it there) to represent all the multiples of 100. Begin again at 0 after 10 children. Ask children to group themselves so that they make a multiple of 10. *Hold up your straws. What number have you made?* Make a display of tens numbers (1 per sheet of paper) using the bundles of straws. They will need to make more bundles to complete all the numbers to 100.

Give pairs of children a set of cards from AS 9 to order and use to practise counting in 10s.

EXTENSION   Adult-led

Give children bags and ask them to fill each with 10, e.g. paperclips. *We know that there are 10 in each bag. How many are there in these 3 bags?* Discuss ways of finding out and elicit that the easiest way is to count in 10s. Repeat for other quantities.

Make a floor number track with tens cards. *How many bags do we need to put on number 10 to make 10 paperclips?* (1) Twenty has 2 bags, 30 has 3 bags.

Plenary

Key idea: We can count in 10s.

1. *How many fingers do Amy, John, and Azir have altogether? What is the quickest way to find the answer?* Count in 10s using tens flashes to find answer. Repeat for other numbers.

2. Look at the straw numbers made by the core group. Ask individuals to hold up the tens numbers in turn as the class counts from 0 in 10s up to 100.

Family activity

● Be a tens detective and spot tens numbers, e.g. house numbers, page numbers, birthday cards in shops, …

Related play activities

● Print a pair of hands to represent 10. Use to make class a number line of tens numbers 10–100.
● Sort objects into groups of 10 and count in 10s.

Counting, reading and writing numbers 12.2 10s from any tens number

Objectives
- count on in 10s from 10, then from any tens number
- count along a large number track numbered only in 10s
- count from a given tens number
- **SP** recognise and recreate simple patterns

Key idea	We can count in 10s from any tens number.

Key words count in 10s, count on (from, to), pattern

You need   number track to 100 (AS G)
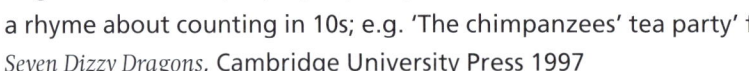
large number cards, 10, 20, … (AS G)

a rhyme about counting in 10s; e.g. 'The chimpanzees' tea party' from *Seven Dizzy Dragons*, Cambridge University Press 1997

IP 8   AS 10

Introduction: oral work and mental calculation

Tens numbers are 'pumpkin numbers': Count round the class in 1s first from 0 and then other small numbers. Whoever reaches a 'pumpkin number' says the number and 'pumpkin' and stands up. Repeat.

Main teaching input and pupil activities

Direct teaching

1. Read 'The chimpanzees' tea party' from *Seven Dizzy Dragons*, Cambridge University Press 1997, or a similar rhyme about counting in 10s. Let children fill in the tens words.

2. *Who can tell me … a tens number? … a tens number bigger than 50? … a tens number less than 40?*

3. Look at IP 8. Begin to count the circles in the border one by one to just beyond 20. *Who knows a quicker way?* Ask a child to point to the tens numbers in the border of the picture and the class to use their fingers to flash tens as everyone counts: *10, 20, 30 … 100.*

4. Point to the washing line at the bottom of IP 8.
    I am going to write 10 in the first space. Who can write the next tens number? Repeat till all numbers to 100 are filled in.

5. Rub out the numbers. *The first number on my tens line this time is 40. What will be the next number? What about the next 3 numbers?* Repeat for different start numbers and vary the length of the sequence without crossing 100.

6. Ask children as whole class, in small groups or individuals to continue the count to 100 from a different start numbers, e.g. start at 40 and count on in 10s to 100, start at 60, count on to 100 …

Pupil activities

SUPPORT ★   Adult-supported
Ask children to arrange large number cards to form a tens floor track. Invite 1 child to stand at the start and to move forwards along the track as others recite the pattern to 100. Repeat from different starting numbers. Challenge children to recite numbers with their eyes shut or by turning over some of the numbers.

CORE   Adult-led

Draw some trains with carriages. Write a tens number on the first carriage so that the last number is 100, e.g. a train with 7 carriages will have first labelled 40. *Look at the tens train. What numbers shall I write on the other carriages?* (50, 60, 70, ...) *How do you know?* (count in 10s) Ask children to help you fill up the other trains with numbers.

EXTENSION   Independent   AS 10

Children work in pairs with 1 sheet of carriages. Cut them out and arrange them to make tens trains with at least 3 carriages, stick on coloured paper and draw engines. You could challenge children to make as many as possible (5) or 4 trains with 3, 4, 5, and 6 carriages.

Plenary

Key idea: We can count in 10s from any tens number.

1. Look at the trains made by the extension group. *Are the tens numbers in the right order? Which trains have 40 on them? ...* Use the train examples to count in 10s from a given 10 to another given 10.

2. Invite 1 or 2 children from extension group to challenge the whole class, a small group or individual to say the numbers on their train without being able to see it. Child gives the starting number and how many 10s to count on. Encourage children to use their fingers to keep track of the 10s as they count on.

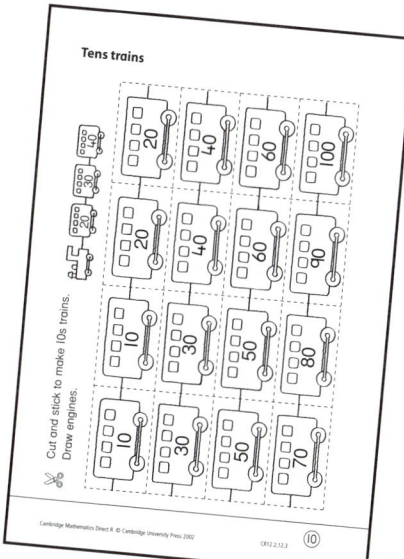

Tens trains

Family activity

● Practise counting forwards in 10s to 100.

Related play activity

● Make '10s' necklaces or snakes by threading 10 beads of one colour then 10 of another. Children could also use any other type of linking construction, eg. chain links. Challenge them to make a 100 snake.

Counting, reading and writing numbers 12.3 Counting back in 10s

Objectives
- count back in 10s from any given tens number
- count back along a large number track numbered only in 10s
- count from a given tens number and stop at another; e.g. count back in 10s from 70 and stop at 10
- **SP** recognise and recreate simple patterns

Key idea | We can count back in 10s.

Key words count back (from, to), pattern, count in 10s

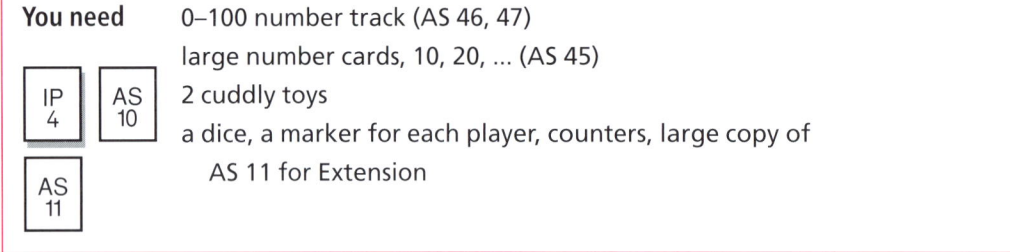

You need 0–100 number track (AS 46, 47)
large number cards, 10, 20, … (AS 45)
2 cuddly toys
a dice, a marker for each player, counters, large copy of AS 11 for Extension

Introduction: oral work and mental calculation

Draw 3 circles with one above the other two. Write a set of numbers in the top circle. Label the bottom circles 'tens number' and 'not a tens number'. Invite children to come and sort numbers into the circles by copying them.

Children show thumbs up or thumbs down each time. Ask for more numbers for both sets.

Main teaching input and pupil activities

Direct teaching

1. *Start at zero. Count forwards in 10s to 100.* Record the tens vertically as children recite.

2. Draw a rocket outline with number 10 on it. *This is a very special rocket. It will not take off if the countdown goes from 10 to zero but only if the countdown starts at 100 and goes down in 10s to zero. Do you think you can make the rocket take off?* Help children by pointing to the tens numbers from bottom to top: *100, 90, 80 … zero BLAST OFF! Which way did we count?* (back)

3. Look at IP 4. *Find the tens numbers. Who can point to the numbers as we count back from 100 in 10s?* Invite a child to do this. *Can you describe the pattern of the numbers?* (above each other, … all in the same line, …)

4. Ask children to help you make a number track on the floor with large number cards: hand them out in reverse order. Invite a child

to choose a number and stand on it. *Martha is standing on 60. Can we count back to zero from 60? 60, 50, 40, … zero.* Repeat from different numbers. Give children opportunities to count back as a whole class, as part of a small group or as an individual. Extend to placing a marker on 1 number while a child stands on a bigger number. Children count back between the 2 numbers, e.g. from 80 to 30.

5. Write sequences of tens numbers on the washing on IP 4: start with 100 but miss some out. *Who can say the pattern and include the numbers that are missing?*

6. Finish by all counting back quickly from 100 to 0. Write the numbers on the washing as children say them, for use with the core activity.

Pupil activities

SUPPORT ★ Adult-led
Use large tens cards to make a floor number track. Ask children to count back from 100 to 0.

Turn over 1 of the cards, e.g. 60 and ask the children to recite numbers again including the missing number. Ask children to suggest which number should be turned over next. Recite the count. Repeat, turning over 1 more card each time.

Place a large toy beside 1 number on the track. Ask children to count back to zero from this number. Repeat for other numbers. Place 2 toys alongside 2 numbers and ask children to walk and count back from the higher to lower number.

CORE   Independent   AS 10

Ask children to work in pairs to cut out carriages and make tens trains that count down from the engine, e.g. 100, 90, 80 or 60, 50, 40, 30. They then stick them on paper and draw engines in front of the greater number. Have the sequence of numbers from 100 to 0 on IP 4 in view for children to refer to if needed.

EXTENSION   Adult-supported   AS 11

Use a large copy of AS 11 so that children can play the track game as a group. Each child chooses a marker and places it on any space on the board. The children can move around the board on the shaded areas in any direction.

Children take it in turns to throw the dice and move that number. If they land on: 'treasure', they receive a counter; ... 'miss a go', they miss their next turn; ... a 'blank', nothing happens; ... a pair of 10s, they count back from the highest to the lowest number. If this is done correctly, they receive a counter. The winner is the person with the greatest number of counters after a set number of turns or time.

Plenary

Key idea: We can count back in 10s.

1. Ask the extension group to show their game. Play a few turns with children all helping with counting back.
2. Say counting back sequences of tens numbers with one missing, e.g. 80, 70, 50, 40. *What's the missing number?*

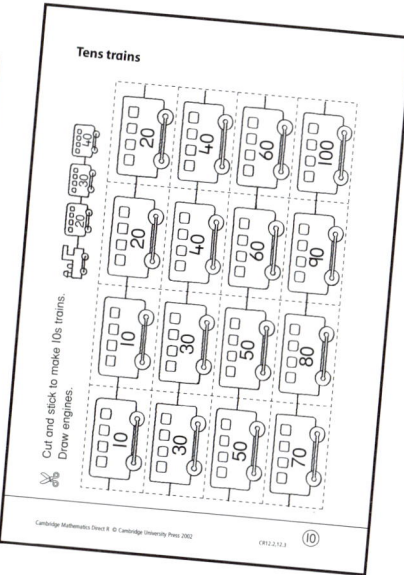
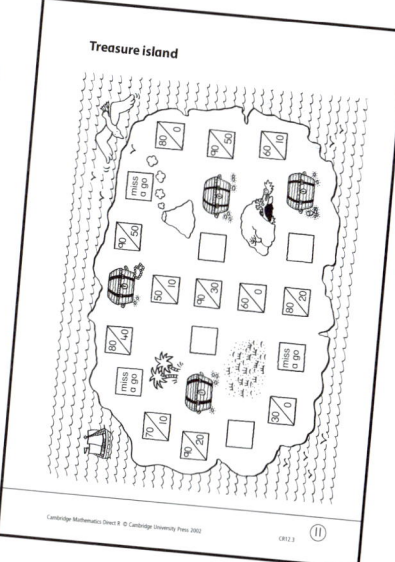

Family activities

- Practise counting backwards in 10s from 100.
- Play the game at home.

Related play activity

- Play track game 'Treasure island'.

Counting, reading and writing numbers 13.1 Saying every other number

Objectives
- count in 1s, but say every other number in a whisper
- look at and point to a number track; saying every other number starting at 1; saying every other number starting at 2
- **SP** recognise and recreate simple patterns

Key idea	We can say every other number name when we count.

Key words   odd, even, every other, pattern

You need	large 1–100 number cards
IP 4 AS 12	cards with 'odd' and 'even'
	floor 1–20 number track
	2 large set circles or hoops
	small 1–20 number cards (AS 41, 43)

Introduction: oral work and mental calculation

Use number cards 1–20 in random order. Ask children to say the number that is 1 more or 1 less than the number shown. If children are confident extend to numbers over 20.

Main teaching input and pupil activities

Direct teaching

1. *We are going to count from 1 to 20 a special way. Whisper the first number and then say the next number in a normal voice, whisper, say, ...* Ask children to try hard to keep the pattern going till they get to 20.
2. Have IP 4 to hand. Repeat the whisper count and record 2, 4, 6, ... on shirts at the top of IP 4.
3. Cover the numbers greater than 20 on the 100 square. *Which number is on the first shirt?* (2) *Who can come and draw a ring around number 2 on the number square?* Repeat with numbers to 10. *We have made a pattern with the numbers that have a ring round them.* Explain that 'every other' number has been ringed. *Who can continue the pattern of rings?* Invite children to come and circle every other number. Talk about patterns children may see, e.g. similarity of first and second lines.
4. *The numbers that we have ringed are a special set of numbers called 'even' numbers.* Write the word

for children to say. *Who can tell me something about the numbers on the shirts?* (same as the ringed numbers, even numbers) *Let's say the even numbers. Remember to say every other number starting at 2.* Hop along the number square as children say 2, 4, 6, 8, 10 ...

5. *Look at the numbers in the number square that we did not ring. They are called 'odd' numbers.* Write the word 'odd' for children to say. *Who can tell me the starting number this time?* (1) Whisper every other number: 1, 3, 5, 7, 9, ... Repeat in an ordinary voice.

Pupil activities

SUPPORT ★   Adult-led

Look at IP 4. Recap Direct teaching **3.–5.** *Who can tell me an even number (with a ring)? ... an odd number (without a ring)?...* Put out a floor number track to 20. *Can you walk along the number track stepping on every other number?* Tell children to start on 1 and say the odd numbers loudly as they step on them. *You can whisper the in between numbers if you want to or say them in your heads.* Repeat starting on 2 for the even numbers.

CORE   Adult-supported   IP 4

Place 2 large set circles on the floor and label one odd and one even. Use cards 1–20 in order and ask children to help you to sort them into the circles. Repeat showing the cards to children in random order and asking individual children to come and place the card in the correct set. Refer to IP 4 if needed. *Who can help me put the odd numbers in order.* Remind children that they can whisper count to help find out which one comes next. *Let's say all the odd numbers to 20* (1, 3, 5, ... 19) Repeat for the even numbers.

EXTENSION   Independent   AS 12

Colour in every other number starting at 1. Choose 5 odd and 5 even numbers.

Plenary

Key idea: We can say every other number name when we count.

1. Divide class into 2 groups, one half to whisper odd numbers, other half to say even numbers clearly. Reverse roles. *Which numbers did we whisper?* (odd numbers) *What are the rest called?* (even numbers)

2. Write a short sequence of odd or even numbers, e.g. 3, 5, 7. *Are these numbers odd or even?* Repeat.

Family activity

● Take turns to say every other number name, e.g. child starts with 1, adult says 2, ... Reverse roles so the child says even numbers.

Related play activity

● Count how many children in the class line but with every other child only saying their number aloud.

Counting, reading and writing numbers 13.2 Rhymes in 2s

Objective ● join in rhymes and make up rhymes of your own involving counting in 2s

Key idea We can make up rhymes about twos.

Key words count in twos

You need number rhyme books
pairs of animals
IP 2 IP 4 A5 size booklets with 10 pages for Extension

Introduction: oral work and mental calculation

Whisper count round the class, whispering every other number starting from 1. Remind children that the numbers they have said out loud are called even numbers. Repeat starting at 0 to generate odd numbers. Put the class into 2 teams with 1 side saying odds and the other evens. *Say every other number.*

Main teaching input and pupil activities

Direct teaching

1. *Today we are going to hear rhymes about even numbers.* Look at a 1–20 number track. *Remember we start at 2 and say every other number to say just the even numbers.* Jump in 2s with your finger as children count 2, 4, 6, … *Each jump was a jump of 2 from 2, so we also call these numbers twos numbers.*

2. Show children IP 2. *Which part of the picture do you think is about a twos rhyme?* (Noah's ark) Sing/say the traditional rhyme 'Noah's ark' (in *Seven Dizzy Dragons*, Cambridge University Press 1997) *What is special about the way the animals went into the ark?* (they went in 2 by 2, 4 by 4, 6 by 6, … ; the twos numbers) Use animals to model the rhyme if available.

3. Ask children questions about the rhyme or the picture, e.g. *If 2 bears, 2 sheep and 2 chickens go into the ark, how many animals altogether? If there are 4 sheep on the ark and 2 more get on what will be the total number of sheep?* Encourage children to count on in 2s.

4. Sing 'Eight fat sausages' from *The Big Book of Number Rhymes* or 'Twelve red balloons' from *Seven Dizzy Dragons* or similar rhymes about twos. Discuss whether the rhymes involve counting forwards or backwards in 2s.

5. Try counting from 2 in 2s forwards to 20 and back again as a whole class, in small groups or individually.

6. Model the beginnings of a rhyme for the extension group to finish, e.g.
   20 children on the bus, 2 get off to go to the shops, 18 smile and wave goodbye,
   18 children on the bus, 2 get off…

Pupil activities

SUPPORT ★ Adult-supported

We are going to make a rhyme book about some naughty monkeys/teddies. Use models to tell children about 2 naughty monkeys who were bored and found 2 more friends to make 4 monkeys, then the 4 monkeys were bored and found 2 more friends to make 6, … Record the twos pattern going down a large sheet of paper or on the board. Discuss what the naughty monkeys might be doing. Ask children to suggest activities for each group and record in simple pictures next to the numbers. Make the rhyme, e.g.

2 naughty monkeys knocking at the door, Found 2 friends and then there were 4.

4 naughty monkeys throwing stones and sticks, ...

Allocate a picture to each child. Encourage them to include the correct number of monkeys in their picture. Assemble pictures into book and include a verse opposite each picture.

CORE   Adult-led

Act out '10 green bottles' rhyme with 2 bottles falling down each time and children saying how many remain standing. Brainstorm ideas of different objects that could be standing on the wall. Choose a number of objects that is double the number of children in the group so that each child will be able to draw a picture. Assemble into a large book and add words, '20 ... standing on the wall, 2 fall down and then there were 18 ...'

EXTENSION   Independent

Make own rhyme following same format as in main teaching, e.g. 20 bears in the woods. Give children an A5 size booklet of 10 pages for them to record what happens to 2 bears on each page and the number of bears that are left in the wood after each 2 disappear.

Plenary

Key idea: We can make up rhymes about twos.

1. Share the rhymes made by each group. Discuss whether rhyme counts forwards or back. Ask children to spot the pattern of 2s as the numbers are said showing thumbs up if it is correct.

2. Count forwards and back in 2s to and from 20, as whole class, in small groups and as individuals.

Family activity

● Make own counting in 2s book.

Related play activity

● Record favourite twos rhymes onto tape for the listening corner.

Counting, reading and writing numbers 13.3 Counting in 2s

Objectives
- count in 2s
- colour hops of 2 on a number track to 10 or more
- **SP** recognise and recreate simple patterns

Key idea | It is quicker to count in 2s than one by one.

Key words   count in twos, even, odd, pattern

You need   number rhyme books
cubes or similar objects for counting
[IP 4] [AS 13]   sets of even 2–20 number cards for Support (AS 41, 43)
counting stick and sticky twos numbers

Introduction: oral work and mental calculation

Sing or say a selection of rhymes relating to counting in 2s, e.g. '8 fat sausages' from *The Big Book of Number Rhymes*, 'Noah's ark' and '12 red balloons' from *Seven Dizzy Dragons*.

Main teaching input and pupil activities

Direct teaching

1. Count to 20 but whisper every other number. Start by whispering 1. *Which numbers did we say out loud?* Record numbers said on number shirts at the top of IP 4. *I have recorded every other number.*

2. Use IP 4 with 31–100 covered on the number square. Ask children to come and circle every other number starting at 2. *We can say that 'every other' number has a circle drawn round it.* Recite pattern of numbers starting with 2. *What do we call these numbers?* (even, twos) Say every other number starting at 1. *What do we call these numbers?* (odd numbers)

3. *Saying just every other number can help us to count objects.* Show children a set of 20 objects in a pot. *We can spread out these cubes in a line and count to see how many there are.* Invite a child to come and arrange the cubes. Ask all children to count how many as 1 child points to each cube. *There are 20 cubes and we counted to 20 one by one (in 1s) to find out how many. Let's count the cubes again but say every other number*

in a whisper 1, **2**, 3, ... **20**. *Can you think of a way we could arrange the cubes so we could just say every other number?* Draw out from children that cubes could be arranged in 2s (perhaps in 2 lines). Rearrange and repeat counting just in 2s to 20. *Is it a quicker or slower way to count?*

4. Give children practice in counting groups of objects in 2s by arranging them in 2s first. Initially get children to check answers by counting the cubes again one by one.

Pupil activities

SUPPORT ★   Independent   AS 13
Children colour the twos pattern on the number snake. Give them a set of even number cards to order.

CORE   Adult-supported
Give children opportunities to practise reciting twos numbers from 2 as a small group and individually. Place some of the numbers from the twos pattern on a counting stick, e.g. 4, 6, 12, 16. Now try counting again. Give pairs of children sets of objects to count in 2s. Child A arranges objects and counts in 2s and child B checks by counting in 1s. Reverse roles. Discuss

the ways children have chosen to arrange objects and ensure an efficient method is being used.

EXTENSION   Adult-led

Work as a group and look at an odd number of objects. Invite a child to come and arrange and then count them in 2s. *What happens when we reach the last object? Can we count 2 more?* (no, there's only one) Repeat with other examples of sets with an odd number of objects.

Finish with word problems that require children to visualise what is happening and count in 2s, e.g. *At the baker's they are selling buns in packets of 2. I buy 3 packets how many buns do I have?* Draw pictures of 3 packets of 2 buns to help children visualise what is happening. *We can count in 2s for each packet: 2, 4, 6.*

Plenary

Key idea: It is quicker to count in 2s than one by one.

1. Ask children from the support group to show their snakes. All count in 2s from 2 forwards to 20 and back.

2. Have 2 groups of 18 objects. Ask 2 volunteers to count one group each, one in 2s and one in 1s. *Who was quicker?* Repeat with different numbers and different children.

3. *Who thinks they can count in 2s to 20 with their eyes shut?* Assess a few children.

Family activity

● Look at home to find objects to count easily in 2s; e.g. pairs of shoes, socks, gloves, ...

Related play activity

● Count objects around the classroom by counting in 2s.

Counting, reading and writing numbers 13.4 Counting pairs

Objectives ● begin to understand and use in practical contexts, odd, even, every other, pair
● count pairs; e.g. pairs of children, socks on a line, animals

Key idea | There are 2 in a pair.

Key words odd, even, pair

You need socks for sorting into pairs
washing line and pegs
collection of items that are found in pairs
collection of objects for sorting into pairs
odd and even labels for Support group
story of 'The Elves and the Shoemaker'

Introduction: oral work and mental calculation

What are the numbers in the twos pattern? Record the pattern from 2 to 20. Draw a large circle on board and label it twos. Write a set of random numbers below the circle. Invite individuals to choose 1 of the numbers to write in the set. Ask the rest to put hands on heads if they agree or fingers on noses if they disagree. Repeat until all the even numbers have been chosen. *What else can we call these numbers?* (even) Try the activity with odd numbers.

Main teaching input and pupil activities

Direct teaching

1. *A pair is when we have 2 things that match.* Ask children to hold up/point to a pair of ... hands, ... feet, ... socks, ... eyes, ... children, etc. *Who can think of other things we find in pairs?* (ears, legs, shoes, laces, gloves, ...)
2. Show children socks. *I must sort my socks into pairs. How many socks make a pair?* Ask children to help you make pairs of socks.
3. Peg 3 pairs of socks on the washing line (hanging each pair from 1 peg). *How many pairs of socks are hanging on the line? How many socks are hanging on the line? How shall we count them?* Establish that counting in 2s will be quicker than counting socks one by one. Repeat with other examples.
4. *I have 7 socks in the washing basket. What sort of number is 7?* (odd) *Can I make them into pairs with none left over?* Give children time to answer and to justify why they think yes or

no. *Let's make pairs and see. I have 1 sock left over.* Explain that there is an 'odd' sock because we started with an odd number of socks. *Do you think the same thing will happen for all odd numbers?* Repeat with different odd numbers till children are sure that, whatever the odd number, you will not be able to make an exact number of pairs. *We can make even numbers into pairs with none left over but odd numbers always have 1 left over.*

Pupil activities

SUPPORT ★ Independent

Children work in pairs. Ask them to sort different collections of objects into pairs, count them in 2s and label them odd or even.

CORE Adult-supported

Working co-operatively, children draw round and cut out pairs of hands from card. Hang 4 pairs, each from 1 peg, on the washing line. *How many pairs of hands? How many hands?* Count in 2s. Pose simple word problems to establish if there is an odd or even number, e.g.

Here are 9 hands. Odd or even? Encourage children to put them into pairs. *I have an even number of hands. Will I be able to make an exact number of pairs?* Use cut-out hands to illustrate answers.

EXTENSION   Adult-led

Read the story of 'The Elves and the Shoemaker'. Set simple problems using the setting. Children could use plimsolls to represent shoes, e.g. *There are 3 pairs of shoes on the shelf, how many shoes are there? The elves made an even number of shoes to give the shoemaker exactly 5 pairs. How many shoes did they make? The shoemaker has to make a set of shoes for the spider who has 8 feet. Will he make an odd or an even number of shoes? The 5 legged goblin wants a new set of shoes. Will he have enough shoes if he buys 3 pairs?* Illustrate problems and encourage children to count in 2s to find the answer.

Plenary

Key idea: There are 2 in a pair.

1. Ask children to make predictions, e.g. *I have 7 shoes. How many pairs can I make? Are there any left over?* Ask children to come and make pairs to check.

2. Discuss the odd and even numbers of objects labelled by the support group. Reinforce that an even number of objects will make an exact number of pairs with none left over and an odd number of objects will not.

Family activity

- Help sort the washing and find all the pairs of socks. How many socks? How many pairs can you make?

Related play activities

- Print hands and feet and then sort into pairs.
- Play pairs matching games.

Counting, reading and writing numbers 13.5 Counting objects in 2s

Objectives
- count in 2s
- discuss ways of organising counting so that it is easier to count accurately
- **SP** recognise and recreate simple patterns

| Key idea | It is not always easy to count objects in 2s. |

Key words   pattern, pair, odd, even, count in twos, every other

You need   1–20 number track (AS 46)

IP 4   IP 5

AS 14

counting stick and 1–20 sticky numbers
pot of 20 cubes all the same colour
necklaces made with an even number of alternating coloured beads
groups of objects to count
A3 copy of AS 14 for Plenary

Introduction: oral work and mental calculation

Write a secret number between 0 and 20 on a piece of paper. Have a 1–20 number track in view. Invite children to ask questions to find the secret number, e.g. *Is it more than 10? Is it even? Is it between 12 and 15?* Answer questions 'yes/no', and then cross out the numbers that it cannot be. After 3 questions allow children to guess. Highlight those questions that were helpful in eliminating a large group of numbers. Repeat with a different secret number.

Main teaching input and pupil activities

Direct teaching

1. Count in 2s from 0 to 20. Remind children to say every other number to make the pattern. *What are the numbers called?* (2s, even numbers) Use a counting stick. Ask children to help you stick the even numbers on it. *Who can tell me the end numbers?* Find and fix 2 and 20. Hold up the rest of the sticky numbers randomly and ask children to put thumbs up if they should be included on the stick. *Who can tell me where this number should go?* Encourage children to count on or back from the ends or a near number. Practise counting on and back using the stick and then with eyes closed.

2. Show children a pot containing 20 cubes (all same colour). *Can you estimate how many cubes there are?* Take estimates and then count the cubes one by one as you take them out of the

pot. *Can anyone think of a quicker way to count the cubes?* Return the cubes to the pot and count them again but this time by taking 2 cubes out each time.

3. *We can arrange the cubes to make it easier to count in 2s. If I put all the cubes in 1 line, how can I count them in 2s?* (count every other cube) Model the method and repeat with different numbers of cubes in the line.

4. *Has anyone got another way?* Model laying out cubes in pairs and find how many by counting each pair in 2s. Repeat with different (even) numbers of cubes.

5. Show children a necklace made of beads in alternating colours. Show how you can use the repeating pattern of 2 colours. *The red bead is second, so I am going to touch each red bead as I count in 2s.* Count in 2s to find how many beads. Repeat activity with necklaces of different lengths. Ask children to come to point to the beads as the others count in 2s.

6. Look at IP 5. *Can you see anything that is easy to count in 2s?* (number of boots on the teddies, insects, ...) *Can you explain why?* (because we can see the pairs) *Which things would it be tricky to count in 2s? Why?* Discuss how the arrangement of some objects, e.g. balloons at the top, makes it hard to keep track.

Pupil activities

SUPPORT ★   Adult-led

Practise counting in 2s as a group and individually. Make use of the number track if needed. Develop the direct teaching and ask children to arrange groups of objects so that they are easy to count in 2s. Keep groups to just even numbers.

CORE   Independent   AS 14

Children count objects arranged for easy counting in 2s. The second part of AS 14 requires children to count objects around the classroom, so they will need to decide how to arrange them and may come across odd ones.

EXTENSION   Adult-supported   IP 4

Extend counting in 2s to beyond 20. Identify numbers on the number square on IP 4 by ringing every other number. Count larger groups of objects by counting in 2s. Look at how to include the remaining 1 when counting an odd number of objects.

> ## Plenary
> Key idea: It is not always easy to count objects in 2s.
> 1. Look at second part of AS 14. Ask children to say how they arranged objects to help counting. *Which were easy to count? Did all children have the same answer for different objects?* Check any questions where children's answers differ and see if they can identify where they went wrong.
> 2. Say familiar twos rhymes.

Family activity

● How many shoes do you have? Find out by counting in 2s.

Related play activity

● Sort shoes by how they fasten, e.g. lace-ups, Velcro, buckles, slip-ons, ... How many pairs of each?

Introduction to Comparing and ordering numbers: block CO3

Vocabulary

- when 2 amounts are being compared: *more, larger, bigger, greater, fewer, smaller, less*
- when more than 2 amounts are being compared: *most, biggest, largest, greatest, fewest, smallest, least*

General overview of the topic

Comparing quantities is fundamental to understanding the relationship between numbers. The aim of this block is to further develop comparison and ordering of numbers, and understanding of ordinal numbers. Children are encouraged to use the related mathematical language with increasing confidence.

Comparing and ordering numbers 3: More ordering and ordinal numbers

Children develop their ability to place numbers in order by comparing them. They begin by ordering complete sets of numbers between 0 and 20 by making links between counting and ordering, and progress to ordering a selection of numbers by considering their relative sizes.

Children's understanding of ordinal numbers is extended from describing positions of objects in lines to describing the order of events. They are also introduced to the relationship between cardinal and ordinal numbers.

Before they start, children need to

- understand and use language to compare 2 given numbers and say which is more or less
- find by counting which of 2 collections has more/fewer objects
- know that a number following another number in the counting sequence is bigger
- say the number that is 1 more or less than a given number
- arrange in order a selection of small numbers
- begin to understand and use ordinal numbers in practical contexts

Concepts covered next year include

- comparing pairs of 2-digit numbers to 30, saying which is more or less
- saying the number that is 1 or 10 more or less than any given number within the range 0 to 30
- finding a number between two 2-digit numbers to 30
- beginning to order numbers beyond 20
- understanding and using ordinal numbers to at least 20

Chief misconceptions

- comparing sizes of objects rather than the numbers they represent e.g. 2 is larger than 6 because it looks physically larger; 3 large teddies are 'more' than 4 small toy dogs because they take up more space
- confusing when an item was placed in a line with where it is positioned in the line, e.g. saying the middle teddy is first because the child remembers it was placed in the line before the others

Comparing and ordering numbers 3.1 Ordering complete sets of numbers

Objectives
- arrange in order a complete set of numbers from 1 to 10 or more
- say the number that is 1 more or 1 less than a given number

| Key idea | Counting helps us put numbers in order. |

Key words order, first, next, after, before, smallest, largest, one more, one less, count, right

You need

AS 15

2 bags
large and small 1–20 number cards (AS 41, 43)
birthday cards showing ages 1–5
washing line
pegs
puppet

Introduction: oral work and mental calculation

Place 1–9 number cards in one bag and 10–20 number cards in the second one. Invite 2 children to pick a number each from the 1–9 bag. *Who can read the numbers? Which is the larger/smaller number?* The class counts from the smaller number to the larger one. Repeat several times. Extend to using pairs of numbers from the 10–20 bag. Extend to one child picking from the 1–9 bag and the other picking from the 10–20 bag.

Main teaching input and pupil activities

Direct teaching

1. Stand birthday cards, showing ages 1 to 5, in a non-numerical row. *Let's read the numbers on the cards.* Start at the left-hand end (from children's viewpoint) and read the numbers together. *Are they in the right order? How can you tell?* (no, because they are not in the same order as when we count) *Let's see if we can put the cards in order. I want the smallest number first so which card comes first?* (the one with 1 on) *Why?* (1 is the first number when we count.) Invite a child to come and swap the positions of 2 cards so that 1 is in the right place.

2. Point to the first card. *Which card should come after this one?* (the one with 2 on) *Why?* (2 is the number after 1 when we count.) Invite a child to swap 2 cards so that 2 is in the correct place.

3. Continue until all the cards are in the right order. *Let's read the numbers again. 1, 2, 3, 4, 5. Does that sound right? Yes, all the numbers are in*

the right order, they are going forwards in the same order as when we count.

4. Repeat the above, this time using number cards from 1 to 10 on a washing line. Once the cards are in order, use them to ask questions such as: *Which number is 1 more/less than 4? How do you know?* Establish that, e.g. the number 1 more/less than 4 is the number 1 after/before 4 on the washing line or when we count.

5. *I have another set of numbers to put on my washing line. Read the numbers with me as I put them up.* Hang numbers 3 to 8 in a muddled order on the line. *Are they in the right order? How can you tell?* (no, because they are not in the same order as when we count) *Which number should be first? Why?* (3, because it comes before the others when you count) Invite a child to swap 2 cards to put 3 in the right place. *Which number will be next? Why?* (4, because it is the number after 3) Continue until all the numbers are in order. *Let's read the numbers to check they are all in the right order: 3, 4, 5, 6, 7, 8. The numbers are in the same order as*

when we count. We started with the smallest number and we finished with the largest number.

Pupil activities

SUPPORT ★   Adult-supported

Give each child a set of 1–10 number cards in a muddled order. Children try to sort the cards into the right order. Check the order, helping children to spot errors by encouraging them to read the numbers aloud. *Which number is 1 more/less than …? How do you know?* Then while the child closes their eyes, swap 2 or more cards around. *Which number cards have I moved? Can you put them back in the right places?* Early finishers could repeat the activities using consecutive numbers that do not start at 1 (e.g. 4–8).

CORE   Adult-led

Initially work with the whole group, using number cards and the washing line to develop the main teaching activity to numbers 10–20. See if children are able to arrange numbers in order vertically as well as horizontally. Children then carry out ★ using consecutive numbers in the range 1–20 chosen according to their ability.

EXTENSION   Independent   AS 15

Children choose number cards to match the numbers shown on the first line of socks. They put their number cards in order and record the correct order. They do the same for the second set of sock numbers. Early finishers can choose their own set of five 1–20 digit cards, recording them on the back of the AS, both as a muddled row of socks and in order.

Plenary

Key idea: Counting helps us put numbers in order.

1. Use a washing line with a muddled set of number cards pegged on and a puppet. *Mr Lion has been washing the football shirts for his team.* Ask children to read the numbers on the cards in their muddled order. *Are the numbers in the right order?* (no, because they are not in counting order) Help children order the numbers: *What number should we start with? What comes next? Why?*

2. Ask questions about the ordered numbers (focusing on children who have been working independently): *What number is 1 more/less than …? How do you know?*

3. Use the puppet to model making errors whilst 'ordering' numbers (e.g. reversing the digits of 2-digit numbers when reading them, missing out a number, looking for a smaller number rather than a larger). See if children can spot the errors and tell the puppet what it should do.

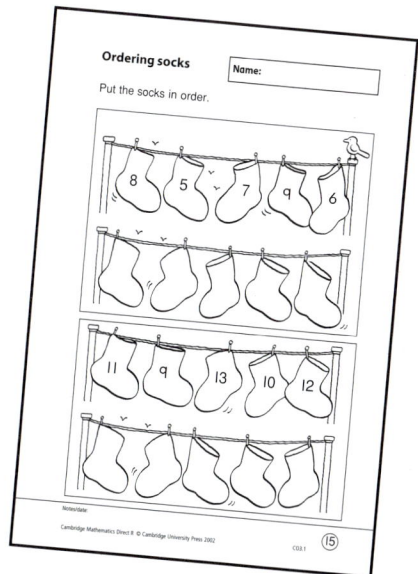

Family activity

*   Child tries to find the numbers 1 to 10 in order around the home, e.g. on pages in a book, a clock, a microwave dial, the TV remote control, …

Related play activities

*   Children number pages of books they make.
*   Children put towers of 1, 2, 3, 4, …. interlocking cubes in order of height by counting cubes. Ask them to predict how many cubes will be in the next tower.

Comparing and ordering numbers 3.2 Ordering numbers

Objectives • arrange in order a selection of small numbers
• know that a number following another number in the counting sequence is bigger

Key idea | To put numbers in order we can keep choosing the smallest number.

Key words order, smallest, first, next, bigger, smaller

You need

AS 16

10 pennies for all
washing line
pegs
large 1–10 number cards (AS 41)
small 1–10 and 1–20 number cards (AS 41, 43)

Introduction: oral work and mental calculation

Give each child 5 pennies. *I go shopping with 5p and buy a biscuit that costs 2p. How much will I have left?* Encourage children to remove 2 pennies and count together 1, 2, 3 to find that 3p is left. Say together: *5p take away 2p is 3p.* Repeat for 'spending' other amounts. Extend to giving each child another 5 pennies so they start with 10p each time.

Main teaching input and pupil activities

Direct teaching

1. Place large number cards 8, 2, 10, 6 and 4 where children can see them, but not on the washing line. *We need to put these numbers in order starting with the smallest. Which is the smallest number here?* (2) *How do you know?* Establish that the smallest number comes before the rest when you count and demonstrate by counting aloud that 2 comes before the other numbers. Invite a child to hang 2 near the left-hand end of the washing line (from children's viewpoint).

2. *To find which number comes next in the order, we are going to look at the numbers that are left and see which is the smallest now. Who can find the smallest number?* (4) Check that all children agree, counting aloud to show that 4 comes before the other numbers. Invite a child to hang 4 on the washing line next to 2.

3. Continue for remaining numbers, each time identifying the smallest number in the remaining group.

4. Ask children to read the numbers in order. *What happens as we go along the line?* (numbers get bigger) *Who can tell me a number on the line that is bigger than 8? How can you tell?* (it comes after 8 on the washing line) *Who can tell me a number not on the line that is bigger than 8? How can you tell?* (any number that comes after 8 when you count is bigger than 8)

5. On the board, draw a washing line with 5 shirts pegged on and a basket (as on AS 16). In your basket write 5 numbers up to 10, e.g. 4, 7, 1, 9, 3. *Teddy wants to hang the football shirts in order on the line. The numbers for the shirts are in the basket. Let's see if we can help Teddy. Which number comes first? Why?* (1, because it is smallest.) Invite a child to write 1 on the first shirt. *I am going to cross out 1 in the washing basket because we have used it. How will we decide which number comes next?* (find the smallest number left in the basket) *So what number comes next?* (3) Ask a child to write 3 on the next shirt and to cross out 3 in the basket (encourage them to make a small cross so that the number can still be read, in case of mistakes). Repeat for the other numbers.

Read through the numbers on the shirts. Ask children to compare the numbers on the washing line, e.g. *Is 7 bigger or smaller than 4? How do you know?* (bigger, because it comes after 4 on the washing line)

Pupil activities

SUPPORT ★ Adult-led

Initially work with children as a group. Reinforce the method of ordering demonstrated during the direct teaching, using the washing line and five 1–10 number cards. Then give each child a shuffled pack of 0–10 number cards and ask them to take 5 cards (some children may be better working with fewer cards to begin with). They try to arrange their cards in order from smallest to largest. *How do you know which card comes next?* Encourage children to find the smallest number in the remaining cards each time, by counting aloud to see which number comes first in the counting sequence. When children have finished, check their work before shuffling the cards and asking them to pick 5 different cards.

CORE Independent AS 16

Children use the AS with sets of 5 non-consecutive numbers between 1 and 15 written in the baskets, according to their ability. They write each set of numbers in order on the shirts on the washing line.

EXTENSION Adult-supported AS 16

Children choose 5 cards each time from a shuffled pack of 1–20 number cards. They record their chosen numbers in Teddy's basket, before writing the numbers in order on the washing line. *How do you know you have put the numbers in the right order?*

Plenary

Key idea: To put numbers in order we can keep choosing the smallest number.

1. Choose 5 children to hold a large 1–10 number card each at the front of the class. Invite individuals to move one child at a time to arrange them in an ordered line. *How do you know that number comes first/next?* Emphasise the method of looking for the smallest number of those remaining.

2. Repeat with different ranges of numbers, including some above 10.

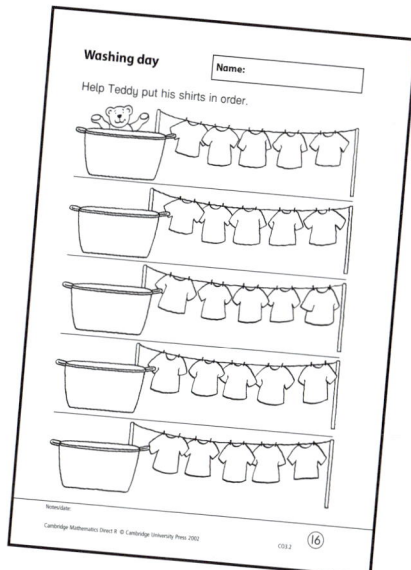

Family activity

- Child orders cups containing up to 20 pieces of pasta, buttons or similar, according to how many objects are in each cup.

Related play activities

- Children order a selection of birthday cards.
- Children order a set of models according to the number of bricks used to make them.
- Children order a set of necklaces according to their number of beads.

Comparing and ordering numbers 3.3 More ordinal numbers

Objective • begin to understand and use ordinal numbers in practical contexts

Key idea | There are special words we can use to say where something is in a line.

Key words first, second, third, ..., tenth, next, between, before, after

You need

AS 17

AS 17 cut into 'cards'
up to about 20 pencils
small pieces of paper
10 different toys
bus stop sign
glue
ordinal number rhyme as described in the Plenary

Introduction: oral work and mental calculation

Briefly show children up to 10 pencils, then hide them. Ask children to guess how many there were and write their answer on paper. Demonstrate counting the pencils to find the exact number. Attach answers on the board in two groups 'close' and 'far away'. Reinforce that a good guess is not just the right number but a close number. Repeat for different numbers of pencils (up to 20).

Main teaching input and pupil activities

Direct teaching

1. Make a line of 10 different toys. Place the 'bus stop' sign at the front of the line. *The toys are waiting at the bus stop for the bus to take them to the park. They are waiting in a line. We use a special word to describe where the toy nearest the bus stop is. We say it is first. Which toy is first? Who can tell me the special word we use to describe the next toy in the line?* Elicit 'second'. *Which toy is second?* Repeat for the other toys in the line.

2. Shuffle the line and ask questions about positions, e.g. *What is third in the line? Where is the teddy in the line?* Each time ask children to explain how they knew, and demonstrate by counting along the line using the 'special' position words in order.

3. Write up the first 5 letters of the alphabet in a line on the board. *Which is the first/second ... fifth letter of the alphabet? Which letter will be sixth/seventh ... tenth?* Write the next 5 letters as they are given.

4. Ask a few more complicated questions about the positions of the 10 letters on the board such as: *Which letter is just after the third letter ... just before the eighth letter ... between the fourth letter and the sixth letter?*

Pupil activities

SUPPORT ★ Adult-supported AS 17
Children need the animal cards cut from AS 17, with the numbers removed. Give instructions to the group to put the first 5 animals in a line, e.g. *Put the snail first ... the butterfly second ...* When the line of 5 is complete, ask children simple position questions, e.g. *Which animal is fourth in the line? Where is the butterfly?* Ask children to put a particular animal (e.g. the ladybird) behind the fifth animal. *Where is the ladybird in the line?* (sixth) Repeat for the remaining animals.

CORE Adult-led
Make a line of 10 toys. Point to the front toy and say, e.g. *The car is at the front of the line. Who can tell me a sentence about where the car is, using one of the special words?* (the car is first in the line) Repeat for several other toys. Ask children to draw

secretly a picture of one of the toys in the line. Children take turns to say a 'special word' sentence to match their picture, e.g. *I have drawn the third toy.* The rest of the group say what each picture must be.

EXTENSION   Independent   AS 17

Children need the numbered animal cards cut from AS 17. They stick them on a piece of paper so the numbers are in the right order. They tell each other where each animal is in their line.

Plenary

Key idea: There are special words we can use to say where something is in a line.

1. Display the work done by the extension group. *Has everyone got the animals in the same order? How do you think they decided which order to put them in?* Discuss how to use counting numbers to stick the animals in order and then 'special' words to describe where each animal is in the line.

2. Ask questions relating to the line of animals, e.g. *What is third in the line? Where is the ladybird in the line? Which animals are next to the frog; Where are they in the line? What is just after the eighth animal ... just before the sixth animal ... between the fifth animal and the seventh animal?*

3. Say a rhyme containing the ordinal numbers in order, e.g. 'The happy clowns' from *Seven Dizzy Dragons*, Cambridge University Press 1997. Repeat, going silent at the ordinal numbers for children to say the words.

Family activities

- A child makes a line of 10 toys. Adult asks child to point to first, third toy, ...
- Adult asks child to describe the positions of letters in written family names using the 'special words', e.g. *Where is the 'r' in Tara?* (it is the third letter)

Related play activities

- When children are in a class line ask them to say which position they are in.
- Ask questions about their position in a class line. *Who is tenth?*
- Ask children to say which letter/word comes first ... second ... in their own writing.

Counting and ordering numbers 3.4 Ordinal and cardinal numbers

Objective • begin to understand the relationship between cardinal and ordinal numbers up to 'tenth'

Key idea	Each special word we use to say where things are in a line goes with a number.

Key words first, second, third, fourth, ..., tenth, last but one, next to last

You need ordinal number rhyme as described in the Introduction
1–10 number track (AS 46)

IP 3 | AS 17 | AS 18

Introduction: oral work and mental calculation

Say an ordinal number rhyme involving actions, e.g. 'The happy clowns' from *Seven Dizzy Dragons*, Cambridge University Press 1997. Choose 10 children to make a line at the front of the class asking each to say their position in the line. Repeat the rhyme going silent at each ordinal number for the class to say the right word. When children at the front hear the clown mentioned that matches their position in the line they do the appropriate action.

Main teaching input and pupil activities

Direct teaching

1. Display IP 3. Point to the clown in the line at the bottom of the IP. *Where is the clown in the line? How did you find out?* Demonstrate counting along using the 'special' position words. Repeat for several other characters in the line.

2. Now ask a few questions such as: *What is sixth ... eighth in the line?* Ask children to explain how they found out. (count along the line)

3. Number the squares below the characters 1, 2, 3, 4, ..., 10. Ask further questions of the type: *What is third in the line?* As characters are identified, establish any links between the names of ordinal numbers and the corresponding cardinal numbers (e.g. **four**th, **four**). Talk about how the numbers in the squares can help you to find the position of the characters in the line.

4. Show the 1–10 number track. Ask questions such as: *What is the third number? Which number is ninth? Where is 7 in the line?* Children demonstrate by counting in ordinal numbers along the number track. Reinforce how most position names match with their number names.

Pupil activities

SUPPORT ★ Independent AS 18
Display IP 3, with the numbers cleared from the boxes below the line of characters. Children need the picture 'cards' cut from AS 18. They stick them on the top part of the AS in the boxes above the cardinal numbers, according to the order shown on the IP.

CORE Adult-supported AS 18
Children need the pictures cut from AS 18. They stick them in the empty boxes on the top part of the AS in the order of their choice. Ask questions about the positions of the characters, e.g. *Where is the big teddy in your line? What is fourth in your line?* Ask children to explain how they decided, encouraging them to make use of the cardinal numbers.

EXTENSION   Adult-led   AS 17

Show an ordered set of pictures from AS 17. Give a range of questions about position, asking children to explain how they can use the numbers to help them, e.g. *Where is the spider in the line? What is fifth? What is between the second and fourth animal? What is behind/in front of the sixth animal?* Extend to questions that include language such as 'last', 'next to last', 'last but one'.

Plenary

Key idea: Each special word we use to say where things are in a line goes with a number.

1. Display a line of pictures from the core group. Ask questions about the positions of the characters, focusing especially on children who worked independently, e.g. *What is seventh in the line? Where is the robot?* Ask children to explain how they decided, emphasising the link with cardinal numbers.

2. Ask questions of the type: *When we count, what is the second number ... the sixth number, ...?*

Family activities

● As child walks down their street they say what colour the front door is on the third house, the fifth house, the tenth house, ...
● As child climbs the stairs, they say *I'm on the first step, I'm on the second step, ...*
● Child places a toy on a stair and describes where it is, e.g. *Teddy is on the fourth step.*

Related play activities

● Ask children to change places in a class line, e.g. *If you are first in the line, go and swap with the person who is eighth. James, go and be seventh.*
● Before children line up to go out to play, give the rules of the 'Lucky position' game, e.g. *The lucky person today will be the fourth person in the line.*

Comparing and ordering numbers 3.5 Using ordinal numbers

Objective	• begin to understand and use ordinal numbers in different contexts

Key idea	The special words we use to say where things are in a line also help us to say the order things happen in.

Key words   first, second, ..., tenth, before, after, last, last but one, next to last

You need	washing line and pegs
AS 19	large 1–10 number cards (AS 41)
	10 different items of washing to match the story you tell
	badges numbered 1–10

Introduction: oral work and mental calculation

Hang a selection of 6 large 1–10 number cards on a washing line in muddled order. Explain that you need to put the numbers in order, from the smallest to the largest. *Which number will we start with? Will the next number be more or less than the first number?* Invite children to sort the numbers and to explain their reasoning. Repeat with other sets of numbers.

Main teaching input and pupil activities

Direct teaching

1. Hang 10 different items (e.g. sock, glove, hat, scarf, handkerchief, T-shirt, shorts, skirt, jumper, cardigan) on the washing line. Read, or make up, a story about items being blown from a washing line by the wind. As each item gets blown away by the wind in the story, remove the matching item from the washing line and attach it to the board, building up an ordered line of items.

2. *We can use our special words for describing where things are in a line to say the order the things blew off the washing line.* Ask questions such as: *What was the fifth thing the wind took? When did the hat go ... first, second, third or fourth?* Ask children to demonstrate their answers by counting *first, second, third, ...* along the ordered line.

3. Ask, e.g. *When did the hat blow away? How many things blew away before the hat?* Demonstrate counting the items before the hat. Emphasise that you are looking at the things before the hat and not including the hat. *How many*

things blew away after the hat? Demonstrate counting all the items after the hat.

4. *What was last thing to blow away?* Establish that the last thing is the same as the tenth thing in this case. *Does anyone know another way of describing the ninth thing to blow away?* Introduce the phrases 'last but one' and 'next to last'.

5. Give out the badges labelled 1–10 to 10 children and ask them to stand in a group at the front of the class. *I want you to imagine that these children have been in a race. Their badges show the order they came in. Who came first, next ... last but one, last? How do you know?* As children are identified, put them into a line.

6. Ask questions about where the children came in the race, e.g. *Where did Rik come? How many were in front of/behind him? Who had 3 people in front of/ behind them?*

Pupil activities

SUPPORT ★ Adult-led

Choose 5 children and have a competition to see who can stand on 1 leg for the longest. As children drop out, stand them in an ordered line, with the winner at the front. Ask questions like: *Who came first? Who was next? What position was that? How many children were ahead of the one who came in third place? Who was fourth? How many were behind fourth place?* Present numbered badges to act as reminders of the links between ordinal and cardinal numbers (they will need to keep these for the Plenary). Repeat with a larger number of children.

CORE   Adult-supported

Children work as a group. They order the 10 washing items on the washing line: with different children choosing the first, second … tenth item. Each child says which position their item takes as they peg it to the line. Ask questions such as: *Which item is first on the line? Which is seventh? How many things are there before/after the seventh item?* Create a wind story, by inviting children to act as the wind taking away one item at a time. Each child says whether their item blows away first, second, … tenth. Put the 'blown away' items in a line in the order they are taken by the wind. Ask questions about that order, e.g. *What did the wind take sixth? How many things had already been blown away? How many were left? What was next to last to blow away?*

EXTENSION   Independent   AS 19

Children make their own story about the wind blowing items off a line. They show the order the wind takes their washing by drawing items in order in the boxes on AS 19 and they complete the labelling of the boxes by writing the appropriate cardinal number. When they have finished, they tell their story to a friend.

Plenary

Key idea: The special words we use to say where things are in a line also help us to say the order things happen in.

1. Ask a few children from the extension group to show their pictures and tell their wind story. Ask other children questions about the story, e.g. *What was the third thing to go from the washing line? What was the fifth item to go from the washing line? If three items had already blown away, which item went next? Where was it in the order?* (fourth)

2. Ask a child from the support group to explain what they were doing. Let each group of children show their badges. Ask questions like: *Who came first? Who came third? Who only had one person in front of them?* Line up children in order, to check.

Family activities

- Child says which clothes they put on/take off first, second, third, … as they get dressed/undressed.
- Child takes shopping from a bag, talking about what they take out first, second … last.

Related play activities

- Hold class races, giving badges, with 1, 2 and 3 marked on them, to children coming first, second and third.
- Children say the order they take toys/pieces of a game out of a box.
- Children use a 'props' box to create their own 'ordered' stories.
- Children talk about what they did that morning, first, second, third.

Adding and subtracting: oral work and mental calculation ideas bank

Using the language of adding and subtracting

- Sit a small group of children as if they are on a bus. Invite another child to get on at the next bus stop. *Are there more or fewer on the bus now?* Repeat for several bus stops, increasing or decreasing the number of passengers.
- Ask children to take a few counters each from a box. *How many have you got?* Ask children to take 2 extra counters. *Has your collection got bigger or smaller? Have you got more or fewer now? Have you added counters or taken them away?* Repeat, asking children to put some counters back in the box.

Combining groups

- Show a number of objects and count them together. Ask a child to add 1 more to the set. *How many have I got now?* Count them all to check. Continue, adding 1 more object each time. When the number becomes too large, start again with a smaller set.
- Count out 3 play biscuits onto one plate: *1, 2, 3*; and 4 onto another plate: *1, 2, 3, 4. How many have I got altogether?* Count them all: *1, 2, 3, 4, 5, 6, 7.* Say together: *3 add 4 is 7.*
- Ask 2 children to take a few apples each and say how many they have. *Put all the apples into this shopping bag. How many are in the bag altogether?* Count them all as a class to check.

Taking away

- Show a number of objects and count them together. Ask a child to take 1 away. *How many are there now?* Count them to check. Continue, taking one object away each time.
- Ask children to count a number of cakes onto a plate. *How many cakes are there?* 'Eat' some of the cakes. *How many cakes are left?* Children count again.
- Show the fingers of one hand 'peeping' over the top of your other hand. *There are 5 birds on the fence.* Fold down some fingers (e.g. 2). *Two of the birds have flown away. How many are left?* Count together to check. Show larger numbers by 'peeping' both hands over a box.
- Sitting in a circle, each child takes a small handful of counting objects and counts

them. Show a 1–4 number card. Each child takes away that number of objects. *How many did you have to start with? How many have you got left?* Children count to find out. See if they can predict this number.
- *Close your eyes. Imagine 4 dots arranged in a square, like they are on a dice. Now take 1 of the spots away. How many are left?*

Counting on or back

- Recite and enact a rhyme that illustrates repeated addition or subtraction of 1.
- A child rolls a large dice and stands on that number (e.g. 5) on a floor number track. *What number is s/he standing on? What number is 1 more than that?* The child takes a step forward along the line to check. Say together, e.g. *5 add 1 is 6.* Repeat.
- Repeat the above activity for subtraction by marking the dice with larger numbers and taking away 1 each time.
- Use a counting stick numbered to 10. *Who can come and point to the number 1 more/less than 5?* Extend to finding 2 more/less.
- Use a floor number track and 2 large dice, one of which shows only the numbers 1, 2 and 3. A child rolls the 1–6 dice and stands on that number. Another child throws the second dice. Before the child on the track moves forward that number of steps, ask: *What number is s/he standing on? What number will s/he reach?* Encourage children to use their fingers to count on. The child on the track then moves.
- *Close your eyes. Imagine you are standing on a number track. You are on the number 5. Now take 2 steps forward. Where are you now?* Continue giving instructions in this way, sometimes carrying on from the current position and sometimes restarting from a new number.

Solving puzzles

- Use 6 biscuits and 2 plates. *How many biscuits shall I put on this plate? So how many will be left for this plate?* Record the split with a drawing and by writing the numerals alongside.

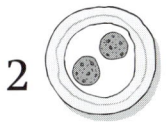 2  4

How else could we put 6 biscuits on 2 plates? Encourage children to find as many different ways as they can. Count the total number of biscuits drawn for each pair of plates to establish that the total is always 6.

- Use dolls and a box as a house. Show, say, 5 dolls and ask the children to count them. *Now shut your eyes.* Put 1 or 2 dolls in the box where they cannot be seen. *Open your eyes. Some of the dolls have gone inside the house. How many can you see outside? So how many are in the house?* Check. Record by drawing a box with 'stick' people outside and inside: label it with numerals. *Let's have a different number of dolls inside ...*

- *Close your eyes. Imagine putting 4 biscuits onto 2 plates. Draw a picture to show how you put your 4 biscuits on the plates. Did everyone do the same?*

Counting how many more are needed

- Sit 6 teddies at a table with 4 cups on it. *There aren't enough cups. How many more do we need?* Invite a child to give out the cups to the teddies and to collect the correct number of cups to complete the pairings.

- Shuffle a set of 1–4 number cards. Turn over the top card and show the number. Children take that number of counting objects. *How many more do you need to make the number up to 5?* Children take the number they think and keep them in a separate group. They check their sets by counting all the objects.

- Children use a number track to predict and then show how many more are needed to make a larger number, e.g. *How many do I need to add to 2 to make 4?*

Finding doubles

- Put some counters on one half of a card ladybird:

This ladybird has lost some spots. There should be the same number on both sides. Who can put on the missing spots? When the spots have been added, ask: *How many spots are there on this side? How many on the other side? How many are there altogether? What is double 3?*

- *Show double 2 with your fingers?* (2 fingers on each hand) *What is double 2?*

- Use a set of large dominoes. Ask children to pick out doubles, e.g. *Who can find the domino that shows double 5? What is double 5?*

- Put doubles dominoes into a bag and pass them around a circle of children. When you say stop, the child who has the bag pulls out a domino and says, e.g. *I have got double 4. Double 4 is 8.* Continue until all dominoes have been used. Collect them and, with the children's help, place them in order. As you point to each in turn, children say 'double 1 is 2, double 2 is 4, ...'.

Using money

- Give children a collection of coins. *Show me a 5 pence coin.* Repeat for other coins, then reverse the activity by holding up a coin and asking children to name it.

- *Take 2 pennies. Now take another 2 pennies. How much have you got altogether?*

- *I want to put 4 pence in my purse. How many penny coins do I need? Is there any other way I could put 4 pence in my purse?*

- *This ball costs 5 pence and the bat costs 4 pence. How much will they cost together?* Children use pennies to count out 5p and 4p, then count them all to find the total. When children are able, encourage them to count on from the first amount to find the total.

- Give each child 6 pennies. *You are going to pay for a biscuit that costs 4 pence. How much will you have left?* When children are able, encourage them to count back from the initial amount to find what is left.

- Use a collection of coins and some items with price labels. *I want to buy this pen. It costs 5 pence. Which coins can I use? Does anyone know another way? If I pay with a 10 pence coin, how much change will I get?*

Vocabulary

- Some children find it easier to picture *counting up* rather than *counting on* and *counting down* rather than *counting back*. It is therefore a good idea to vary the language used.

General overview of the topic

These blocks focus on counting on and counting back, which are important steps in becoming more efficient at adding and subtracting. In earlier blocks, children add by counting out groups of objects, combining them and then counting all the objects. Counting on refines this procedure by reducing the amount of counting that is needed to find a total. In earlier blocks children subtract by counting out the initial quantity, removing the number to be taken away and then counting how many are left. Like counting on, counting back reduces the amount of counting needed to reach an answer.

These blocks also give opportunities for children to apply their counting on and counting back strategies in the context of money.

Adding and subtracting 5: Counting on and counting back
Children develop the understanding that counting on can be used to find totals. They begin by adding objects one by one to a given set and progress to counting on along a number track. Children also begin to count back to find how many are left after some have been taken away.

Children begin to recognise that some coins have greater values than others, and to read and write simple prices. They apply adding and subtracting strategies to find doubles and to solve money problems.

Adding and subtracting 6: Adding and subtracting puzzles
Children apply counting on to find a total when one of two groups of objects is hidden (where the 'counting all' strategy cannot be employed). They develop their ability to count back, and work out, by counting, how many more are needed to make a larger number.

The context of money is used to practise counting on and back. Children begin to choose and use appropriate number operations to solve money problems. They explain orally and, where appropriate, record in their own way how a problem was solved.

Before they start, children need to

- begin to use the vocabulary involved in addition and subtraction
- begin to relate addition to combining two groups of objects and counting the total
- begin to relate subtraction to 'taking away' and counting how many are left
- begin to understand and use the vocabulary related to money
- begin to distinguish coins

Concepts covered next year include

- beginning to use the $+$, $-$ and $=$ signs to record mental calculations in a number sentence
- beginning to recognise that addition can be done in any order
- beginning to recognise that more than two numbers can be added together
- understanding subtraction as 'take away', 'difference' and 'how many more to make'
- beginning to develop mental strategies

Chief misconceptions

- including the starting number when counting on or back rather than beginning with the next number, e.g. when adding 3 to 4 saying 4, 5, 6 rather than 5, 6, 7; when subtracting 4 from 7 saying 7, 6, 5, 4 rather than 6, 5, 4, 3
- including the starting number when counting on or back on a number track
- thinking that the number of coins alone determines their value, e.g. because there are more of them, seven 1p coins must be worth more than one 10p coin
- thinking that the size of coins indicates their value, e.g. because a 2p coin is bigger than the 5p coin it must be worth more

Adding and subtracting 5.1 Adding by counting on

Objectives
- begin to relate addition to counting on when totalling a number of objects
- begin to relate addition to counting on when hopping along a number track

Key idea	Count on to find a total.

Key words   count on, total, add, altogether, how many now?

You need
IP 3   AS 20

number cards 1–10 (AS 41)
bag of sweets
small toys, Blu-Tack
large dice and 1–20 floor number track for Support
1–20 number tracks for all (AS 46)
dice for Extension

Introduction: oral work and mental calculation

Play 'Number claps': Show children a number card and ask them to do that number of claps. Encourage them to try without saying the numbers. Repeat with different numbers and actions, e.g. patting knees, jumping on 2 feet, tapping head, drawing a circle in the air, ...

Main teaching input and pupil activities

Direct teaching

1. *We are going to learn how we can count on to find a total.*
2. Show a bag of sweets. *I have 6 sweets in this bag and I have been given 3 more.* Show the extra 3 sweets. *Can anyone tell me the total number of sweets I've got?* Discuss how total means how many there are altogether. *How many are in the bag already? (6) Let's count them, then count on with me as I add the extra sweets... 7, 8, 9.* Add a sweet to the bag each time you count on 1. *There are 9 sweets altogether.* If necessary, remove all the sweets and count them altogether to check. Repeat for other pairs of numbers beginning with the larger.
3. Look at IP 3. *The stepping stones on this picture make a number track. Can you say the numbers from the beginning of the track to the end?* Write in the missing numbers as children say them.
4. *We are going to use the number track to help us add by counting on.* Use a small toy such as a plastic frog and stick it on stepping stone number 7. *The frog is on number 7. If he hops forwards 4 more on the number track, where will he land? Let's find out.* Ask children to count 1, 2, 3, 4 in their heads as you move the frog. *The frog started on 7, hopped on 4 and landed on? (11) We say '7 add 4 is 11'.* Record the sentence at the bottom of IP 3 and say it all together.
5. Repeat. Invite children to come and move the frog, ensuring they do not begin the count before the frog has hopped.
6. Return to the original bag of sweets, reminding children that there are 6 sweets in the bag and 3 more to be added. *Can anyone tell me how we can use the number track to help us find out how many there are altogether? (start at 6 and count on 3)* Invite a child to fill in numbers in a number sentence and all say 6 add 3 is 9. Repeat with other examples.

Pupil activities

SUPPORT ★   Adult-supported
Use a floor number track to 20. Invite one child to come and stand on 2. Ask another child to roll a large dice and say the number showing.

The first child moves by that number. Say together *2 add 5 is 7*. As they become more confident let children choose which number they start on (14 or less). Give each child a number track and small toy. Ask one child to choose a number less than 10 as a starting number and another to roll the dice for the count on number. Children move their toy along their tracks. Help them to record each one in their own way.

CORE   Independent   AS 20

Children use individual number tracks and plastic toys to help them solve counting on questions on AS 20. They create their own question for the final statement. (Either use a dice or just choose numbers.)

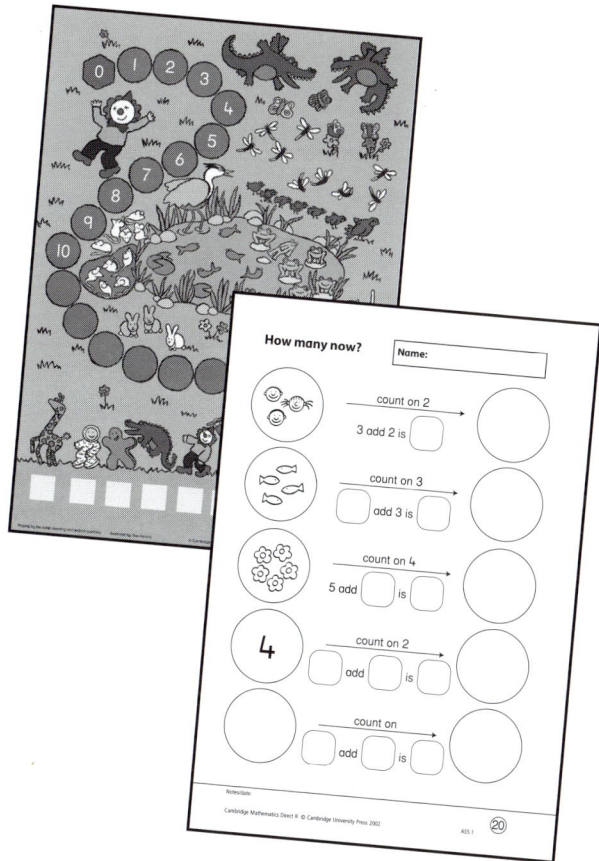

EXTENSION   Adult-led   IP 3

Write up the sentences: 4 count on 3 makes ☐ altogether; 4 add 3 is 7. *What would happen if we did not have any number tracks? Could we still find a total by counting on?*

Show children how to put 4 in their 'heads' and then use 3 fingers to count on 3. As they count on from 4, they bend down one finger for each number said. Use IP 3 to check the first few examples.

Ask children to work with a partner and create their own count on questions by rolling a dice twice. Record each sentence as in Direct teaching. Children try to solve them by counting on in their heads.

Plenary

Key idea: Count on to find a total.

1. *We have been finding totals by counting on. We started with a number, added some more and found out how many we had altogether. Can anyone tell me an important thing we must remember when we count on with a number track?* Elicit things such as placing the toy on the first number, not counting the number you are already on, counting carefully, ... Try a few questions with a number track.

2. *Let's try some counting on problems without using a number track.* Ask children to close their eyes and imagine a number track. *Imagine that I have 8 books on my table. I collect 2 more, how many do I have now?* Discuss the answers they reach and invite children to describe what they could 'see in their heads' as they solved the problem. Ask the extension group to show how to use fingers to keep count. Check using a number track. Repeat for other examples.

Family activities

- Use full and part full packs to set problems such as *There are 6 eggs in this box and 3 more in this box. How many altogether?* Encourage counting on to find the total.
- Give children some counting on problems to solve. Can they challenge you to solve some problems?

Related play activities

- Play track games that involve children in counting on, e.g. 'Snakes and ladders'.
- Find out how many altogether in two sets of toys, shopping, crayons, ... by counting on.

Adding and subtracting 5.2 Doubles

Objectives
- begin to relate the addition of doubles to counting on
- **SP** solve practical problems involving doubling and halving in a real or role play context

Key idea	Count on to find how many altogether in a double.

Key words   double, count on, add

You need   interlocking cubes
counting objects (cubes, counters, buttons, plastic teddies, …)
  0–20 number track (AS 46)

Introduction: oral work and mental calculation

Play 'Conductor counting': Divide the class into 3 or 4 groups. Sit each group in a separate space, making sure that all children can see you. *I am the conductor. When I point to your group it is your turn to count out loud.* Keep the children alert and involved by varying the order in which you select the groups and the amount of counting each group does. Agree to stop counting on a given signal or when a given number is reached. Repeat the counting, starting with a different number each time.

Main teaching input and pupil activities

Direct teaching

1. *Can anyone tell me what 'double' means?* Discuss contexts where children meet the word, e.g. using 2 dice in a board game and throwing the same number on each. *How many fingers on one hand?* (5) *How many altogether on two hands?* (10) *We can say '5 add 5 is 10' or 'double 5 is 10'.*

2. *Let's use cubes to make doubles.* Invite 2 children to take 4 cubes each and make a tower with them. *Both towers are the same. They both have 4 cubes. If Anita gives her tower to Marco, then Marco has double the number of cubes.* One child gives their cubes to the other. *How many cubes has Marco got now? Start at 4 and count on 4 more …5, 6, 7, 8.* Ask children to tell you the total. (8) *4 add 4 is 8 cubes. Double 4 is 8.* Ask Marco to give back half his cubes.

3. Look at IP 9. Discuss what children can see. *Who can see some mice?* Draw another mousehole with 1 mouse inside and 1 mouse outside. Write 1 (mouse) 'in' and 1 (mouse) 'out'. *If 1 mouse is in his hole and one mouse is outside, how many mice altogether?* (2) Record 'double 1 is 2' and ask children to say the sentence. *Half of the mice are in the hole. Half of 2 is 1.* Repeat for double 2 (half of 4) and double 3 (half of 6). *This time there are 8 mice altogether. Half of the mice are in the mousehole. Who can draw them?*

4. Ask some other doubles problems, e.g. *On Monday the mice have 5 pieces of cheese. On Tuesday father mouse goes out and collects some more cheese so that they have double the amount. How many pieces of cheese are there now?* Establish that you need to find the double of 5. *We can start at 5 and count on another 5.* Show children how to use their fingers to keep track as you count 6, 7, 8, 9, 10. *Double 5 is 10 so there are 10 pieces of cheese altogether.* Repeat with other examples.

Pupil activities

SUPPORT ★   Adult-supported

Use children to make doubles: Ask 2 children to stand in one group and 2 children to stand in another. *2 and 2 is the double of 2. What is the double of 2 altogether?* Model the language as you point to the children: Start with 2 children, count on 2... 3, 4. *Double 2 is 4.*

Ask children to use counting objects to show doubles by making two groups with the same number in each. Encourage them to find out 'how many altogether' by counting on from the number in the first group, using the objects in the second group to help. Children record doubles in their own ways using pictures, words or numbers.

CORE   Adult-led

Read the rhyme 'Twelve little monkeys' from *Seven Dizzy Dragons*, Cambridge University Press 1997, or another rhyme/story about halving numbers. Illustrate what is happening in the rhyme by using cubes. Have 12 cubes to represent 12 monkeys. *How can we find half of 12?* Elicit that we need to make 2 groups the same size. Ask children to help you separate the cubes. Check each attempt by counting together until the groups are the same size. *Half of 12 is 6.* Ask children to work in pairs and repeat for other numbers from the rhyme. Encourage them to explain orally how they are working out halves of numbers and record in their own way.

EXTENSION   Independent   AS 21

Children join in with the core activity and then investigate doubles and halves with dice.

Plenary

Key idea: Count on to find how many altogether in a double.

1. *What does double mean?* Ask a child from each group to explain. Recap the meaning of double as how many in 2 groups of the same number. Ask individuals to find doubles of a variety of numbers. Look for the use of counting on. Encourage children to show you 2 equal jumps on a number track.

2. Read 'Twelve little monkeys' again.

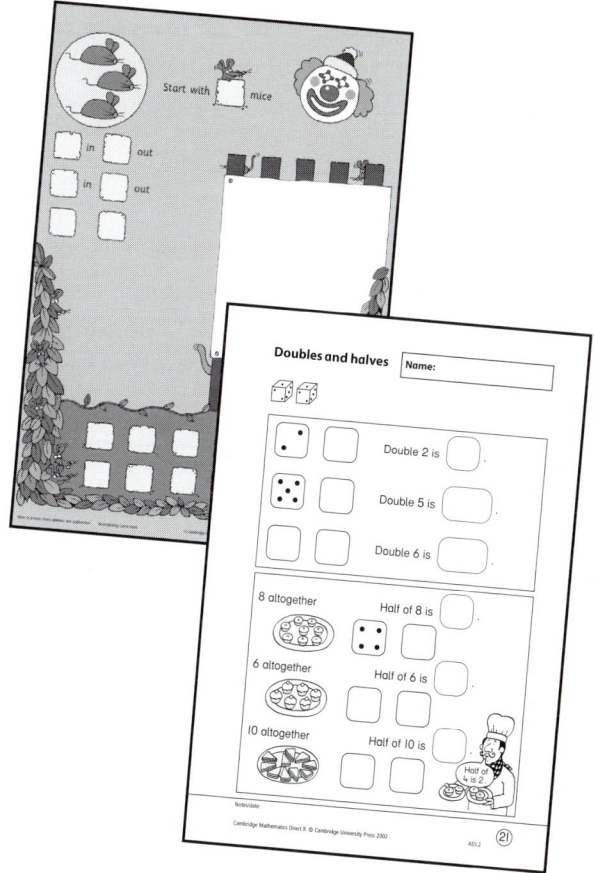

Family activities

- Use pairs of socks, gloves, shoes, ... to work out doubles.
- Use situations where 'two lots' are involved to work out doubles:
  1 sandwich, 2 slices of bread. How many slices for 2, 3, 4, 5 sandwiches.
  There are 4 cakes in a packet and we've got two packets. How many cakes have we got altogether?

Related play activities

- Make sets of shorts and tee-shirts from paper. Children print, paint or stick on spots or other shapes so that there is the same number on top and bottom thus making a double.
- Find the 'doubles' in a set of dominoes.

Adding and subtracting 5.3 Counting back

Objectives
- remove a smaller number from a larger and find how many are left by counting back from the larger number
- **SP** choose and use appropriate number operation to solve 'story' problems involving money
- **SP** explain orally, and where appropriate, record in own way how problem was solved

| Key idea | Count back to work out how much is left. |

Key words   count back, how many are/much is left/left over?

You need

floor 0–20 number track
0–20 number tracks for all (AS 46)
cubes, large dice
cards with amounts 5p to 15p for extension

Introduction: oral work and mental calculation

Play 'Dice roll': Place a floor number track where all children can see it. Choose a number and select a child to stand on this number. Choose another child to roll the dice. Ask all children to say the number that is rolled. Ask the child on the number track to move forwards that number of spaces. Challenge the remainder of the children to use their fingers to show which number the child will land on before they reach it. For numbers greater than 10 children can show all 10 fingers quickly as a 'tens flash' and then the number of fingers for the remaining amount. Repeat with different children on the number track and rolling the dice.

Main teaching input and pupil activities

Direct teaching

1. Write the numbers 18, 19 and 20 on the last 3 stepping stones on the number track on IP 3. *This path has some numbers on it, but there are some missing. Let's count back along the number track 20, 19, 18 ... what comes next?* Carry on in this way, filling in the missing numbers on number track. Give children practice in counting back from different numbers. Ask different groups to count back from different numbers.

2. Point to the line of characters at the bottom of IP 3. Count them together to find that there are 10. *Four of the creatures run away.* Cover the last 4 characters. *How many are left?* (6) *How do you know 6 are left?* (counted them) *Two more run away.* Cover next 2 characters. *How many are left now?* (4)

3. *We can count back on the number track to work out*

how many are left. Point to the full line of creatures and cover over 4. *What happens when 4 run away from 10?* Ask children to look at the number track as you start at 10 and count back 4. Show children how to use their 10 fingers to keep count of how many they are counting back by bending down one finger at a time as each number is said ... 9, 8, 7, 6. *How many are left?* (6)

4. Repeat for other examples with small numbers, covering characters at bottom of picture and using the number line to help counting back. Encourage children to show how many to count back with their fingers and to bend them down as they count down.

5. Pose some story problems to solve (model each one using cubes, coins, ...), e.g. *I have 6 biscuits on a plate. If I eat 4, how many are left? I have 8p. I give 4p away. How much have I got now?* Ask individuals to help you solve the problem on the number track and use fingers as before.

Pupil activities

SUPPORT ★ Independent   AS 22

Count back on number tracks.

CORE   Adult-led

Give more examples as in Direct teaching **5**.
Encourage children to count back using their
fingers with the number track at first. Observe
children as they do so, checking they are all
counting back correctly and not including the
number they are starting on. Ask children to
solve 2 problems with or without a number
track, record in their own way and explain to
their partner how they found the answer.

EXTENSION   Adult-supported

Use a pack of cards showing amounts between
5p and 15p. *We are going shopping at the 'five pence
shop' where everything costs 5p.* Invite a child to
take the top card and read out the amount, e.g.
9p. *You have 9p and spend 5p. How much will you
have left?* Encourage children to show 5 fingers
and to bend down one finger at a time as they
count back 5. Repeat with different children,
asking them to work out the answer on their
own and then checking to see that all children
reach the same answer. Watch out for children
who have an answer 1 more than the correct
amount as they have probably included the start
number in their count. Choose a child to
explain how they counted backwards.
Repeat as above but vary the amount spent in
the shop. Ask children to record three of the
problems in their own way.

Plenary

Key idea: Count back to work out how much
is left.

1. Play 'Count back': Ask a child to choose a
    number from 1 to 10 that is more than 6
    and tell the class, e.g. 8. Ask another child
    to roll a dice. All children say the number
    it lands on, e.g. 4. *What is 8 take away 4?
    Count back 4 from 8.* To make the game
    competitive, divide the class into 2 teams
    that take turns to answer questions. Give
    a point for each correct answer.
2. Extend to numbers to 15 if appropriate.

Family activity

- Use situations where things are 'taken away' to practise the counting back method:
  There were 8 chocolate wafers in a pack. Three have been eaten, how many are left?
  There were 6 eggs in the box. We used 4 in these omelettes. How many are left?
  You had 10p. You have just spent 4p. How much have you still got?

Related play activity

- Set up a class shop with activities that involve children counting backwards, e.g. starting with a
  certain amount, spending and finding what is left.

Adding and subtracting 5.4 Reading prices

Objectives
- **SP** use coins in role play
- begin to relate addition to counting on when totalling a number of objects
- remove a smaller number from a larger and find how many are left by counting back

Key idea | Prices tell us how much to pay.

Key words price, cost, pay, change, how much is left?

You need
IP 6   AS 23

cubes, large container, digit cards for all
purse containing real coins: 1p, 2p, 5p, 10p, 20p, 50p, £1, £2
Blu-Tack
'purses' containing ten 1p coins/ten £1 coins for Support
'purses' containing six 1p coins and two 2p coins for Core
'purses' containing a total of 15p/20p for Extension
shop items (real or drawn on cards) with prices up to 5p (or £5)

Introduction: oral work and mental calculation

Play 'Cube drop': Drop a few cubes one by one into a container without children being able to see. Children listen and count silently as the cubes are dropped. They show how many they think are in the box using fingers or digit cards. Choose one child to come and count the cubes in the box to establish the correct answer. Repeat.

Main teaching input and pupil activities

Direct teaching

1. Look at IP 6. *I have some money in my purse. Can you match my coins to their pictures?* Ask a child to choose a coin. *What colour is it? What shape is it? Can you see a number on it? Who knows what coin this one is? Can you match it to the picture?* Blu-Tack the coin on top of its picture on the IP. Repeat. *Discuss how there is no match for the £2 coin:* Blu-Tack it below the £1.

2. Point to a gingerbread man. *I am going to write the price of the gingerbread man on a label. The price tells us how much the gingerbread man costs, how much we need to pay if we want to buy one.* Explain that the price of the gingerbread man is 4 pence. *What number shall I write?* (4) *Then I write a 'p' to tell me it is 4 pence.* Give a child a purse containing 1p and 2p coins. *Show me which coins you can use to pay. Are there any other ways?* If children choose to use one

or more 2p coins encourage them to start with the 2p coin and count on 3, 4 as they add pennies or another 2p coin. Repeat.

3. *Who would like to choose 2 things to buy from the shop?* Record the 2 items chosen in the empty circle. Ask children to tell you the prices making sure they include pence. *Do you know how much altogether?* Record the appropriate amounts with the word 'add', e.g. 4p and 3p. *Let's use pennies to help.* Ask the child to count out the correct number of 1p coins for each item. *We have 4p here. Start with 4 and count on 3 to find how many altogether.* Remind children to keep track of how many they have counted on with their fingers. Repeat with other examples.

4. *Simon, you are going to go to the shop with 10 pennies to buy a cake.* Give him a purse containing ten 1p coins and ask him to hold them up one by one for the class to count. Choose a child to be shopkeeper and ask Simon to pay for a cake. *How much do you think*

is left in Simon's purse? How do you know? Let's check by counting back. Start at 10p and count back the amount spent together, using fingers. Check that it matches the amount in the purse. *What else could Simon buy?* Repeat with other examples.

Pupil activities

SUPPORT ★   Adult-led

Have a selection of items for children to buy. Invite children to each choose one item to buy. *How much do you have to pay?* Children match the correct number of 1p coins for the item.

Then give each child ten 1p coins and ask them to buy 2 items. *How much do you have to pay altogether?* Help children to count on from the first amount to find the total. *How much money have you got left? Can you buy any thing else?*

The activity could be repeated as a pound shop, with children going shopping with ten £1 coins.

CORE   Adult-supported

Help pairs of children to act as shopkeeper and customer by modelling each activity first. Encourage children to count on. Customers need purses with six 1p coins and two 2p coins:

- The customer chooses an item, the shopkeeper tells them the price and the customer chooses a coin or coins to pay. Swap roles.
- Repeat with 2 items. The customer asks *How much altogether?* Before they pay, ask children to predict how much they will have left by counting back.
- Ask the customer to choose something else to buy using the remaining money. *Have you got enough money left?* Children may now not be able to make the exact amount needed with their coins. Encourage them to give more and receive change.

EXTENSION   Independent   AS 23

Give children 15p or 20p in familiar coins. Fill in an appropriate range of prices on AS 23 before copying it. Children choose 2 items to buy and work out how much they need to pay. They choose how to record the total cost and how much they have left. Repeat.

Plenary

Key idea: Prices tell us how much to pay.

1. Show an item. *How much did I spend? What coins do you think I used to pay?* Ask a child to show you with coins. *Are there any other ways?* Repeat.
2. Now choose 2 items. *How much did I spend altogether? How do you know? If I had 10p/12p/15p to start with, how much have I got left?*

Family activity

- When at the shops look for the prices of different items (small, whole numbers of pence or pounds). Ask children to try and tell you how much the various items cost.

Related play activities

- Make lists/pictures of items for children to buy at the class shop.
- Make items for a class baker's shop out of salt dough.

Adding and subtracting 5.5 Paying with coins

Objectives
- **SP** use coins in role play
- **SP** begin to recognise some coins have a greater value

Key idea | We can pay 5p with five 1p coins or one 5p coin.

Key words price, cost, pay

You need

IP 6	AS 23
AS 24	

a purse containing 1p, 2p, 5p, 10p, 20p, 50p, £1 and £2 coins
dice, dominoes, cards with totals for dominoes
a glove puppet
a varied collection of coins for sorting for Support
a collection of 1p, 2p, 5p coins for Core
a collection of 1p, 2p, 5p, 10p, 20p coins for Extension
Blu-Tack

Introduction: oral work and mental calculation

Play 'Domino match': Give half the class a domino each and the rest a card with numbers corresponding to the total number of spots on each domino. On the command 'go' children find a matching partner and sit down. When all children have found their partners, ask a few pairs to show their dominoes and cards. Ask pairs to say the numbers at each end of their domino and the totals. Highlight the doubles.

Main teaching input and pupil activities

Direct teaching

1. Look at IP 6 and name the coins. *I want to find a 2 pence coin in my purse.* Encourage children to give the features of the coin. Invite a child to pick a 2p coin from your purse and Blu-Tack it to its picture. Repeat for other coins (stick the £2 coin under the £1 coin).

2. Show children two 1p coins. *How much money do I have?* (2 pence) *Who can see one coin we can use instead of these two 1p coins?* (2p coin) Give the two 1p coins to a child. *Let me give you one coin instead.* Take back the 1p coins and hand over a different 1p coin. *Is that fair?* (No) *Why?* (it's only 1p and I had 2p before, ...) Give a 2p coin instead and check that children are happy that they can use either two 1p coins or one 2p coin to buy something that costs 2p. Repeat similarly for a 5p coin.

3. Play 'Which would you rather have?': Show children 2 different coins and use a puppet to ask them which they would choose for the puppet if they wanted him to have the most money. Give the puppet the chance to make the wrong choice, e.g. I want this 2p coin because it is bigger than the 5p coin and will buy more. *Do you agree?* Demonstrate by exchanging for 1p coins.

4. Develop the activity to include numbers of coins, e.g. *I am going to choose eight 1p coins rather than the 20p coin because then I will have more coins so I will have more money. Am I right?* Give children opportunities to explain their thinking.

5. Write prices less than 10p on items on IP 6. Blu-Tack some coins to use on the circles in the middle of the picture: include only two 1p coins, several 2p coins and a 5p coin. *What coins do I have? What is the price of the bread roll?* (e.g. 3p) *Is there a 3p coin?* (No) *So what shall we do?* Hear ideas. Establish that one 2p coin and one 1p could be used as 2 and 1 makes 3 (so 2p and 1p makes 3p). Repeat with other

amounts. Record by drawing round the coins and writing their number on them.

Pupil activities

SUPPORT ★ Adult-led

Use a muddled collection of coins:

- Ask children to sort them into sets of the same type.
- Match 2p, 5p, 10p and 20p coins with the correct number of 1p coins. Compare the numbers of matching 1p coins. Question children to make sure they understand that the size, shape or colour of a coin alone does not determine the value of the coin. The 20p coin has the most 1p coins matching it but it is not the largest coin in the collection.
- Use combinations of 2p and 1p coins to make amounts up to 20p.

CORE Independent AS 23

Write some prices between 5p and 10p for the items on AS 23 before copying it. Children see how many different ways they can make the amounts using combinations of coins. They record their work by drawing around the coins and writing the value on each.

EXTENSION Adult-supported AS 24

Play a coin exchange game in pairs. Each child has AS 24. They take turns to roll a dice and take that number of pennies to place on the 1p spaces. When they have five 1p coins exchange for a 5p coin. Take on the role of banker and ensure children are exchanging correctly. Encourage children to say, e.g. *Please may I exchange my two 5p coins for one 10p coin, ...* The winner is the first child to get one 20p coin.

Plenary

Key idea: We can pay 5p with five 1p coins or one 5p coin.

1. Indicate a collection of 1p and 2p coins. *If I use 2 of these coins, what is smallest amount I can make?* (2p) *And the most I can make?* (4p) Ask a child to demonstrate. *Are there any other amounts I can make? What if I use 3 coins?* Ask individuals to come and pick up any 3 coins. Record and find the totals.

2. *This jam tart costs 5p. I have 3 coins that make 5p. Can you think what they are?* Discuss ways to solve this. Repeat with other amounts and discuss how the same amount can be made with a different number of coins.

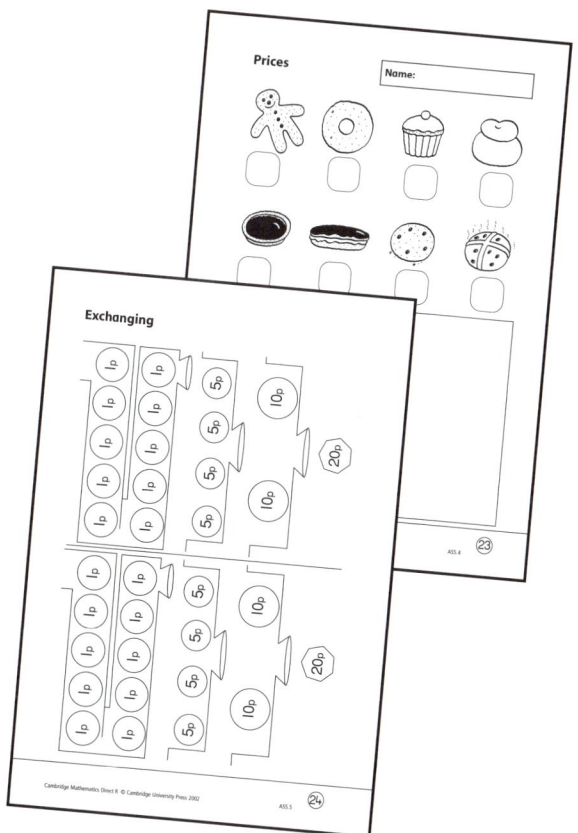

Family activity

- Look at the coins that an adult has at home or when they are given change in a shop. Can you say what they are?

Related play activities

- Use empty packets and make price labels for them in a class shop. Challenge children to use different combinations of coins to pay for items from the shop.
- Play 'Banks': Have a muddled collection of coins for sorting into their correct 'compartments' in a coin tray or till.

Adding and subtracting 6.1 Finding totals by counting on

Objective ● find a total by counting on when one group of objects is hidden

Key idea Count on to find a total even if some things are hiding.

Key words total, altogether, add, count on

You need post box, 10 letters
1–20 number tracks and cubes for Core group (AS 46)

IP 3   AS 25

Introduction: oral work and mental calculation

Play 'Missing claps': *I am going to choose a total number of claps. It's, e.g. 7. Now I am going to start clapping. Count in your heads how many claps I do. When I stop and point to you, take over the claps until you reach 7 altogether.* Set a rhythm with your claps and then point to children for them to continue to 7. Repeat for different bonds and totals.

Main teaching input and pupil activities

Direct teaching

1. Look at IP 3. Ask children to count along the track as you point to each number to 10 and carry on to 20 as you write in the numbers. *What animals can you see in the picture? How many frogs are there?*

2. *There are some more animals who are hiding today. I wonder if we can find how many there are altogether.* Pose a problem, e.g. *There are 7 goldfish hiding under the water. How many others can you see?* (5) *Let's use the picture to help us find how many altogether. We know that there are 7 goldfish under the water that we can't see, so we need to start from 7 and count on the ones we can see.* Say 7 and then point to the goldfish as the class counts on: *8, 9, 10, 11, 12. So what is the total number of goldfish?* (12) *7 add 5 is 12.*

3. Write: 7 add 5. *Who can use the number track to help us add the numbers.* Help a child to use a small toy or counter to show counting on 5 from 7 along the number track. Draw 'hops' for each of the 5 jumps. Record 7 add 5 is 12 at the bottom of the picture.

4. Repeat **2.** and **3.** with other animals, keeping the hidden group larger so that the smaller number is counted on, e.g. 5 rabbits are in the burrow and 3 out looking for food, 3 herons are in the nest and 1 is in the pond catching some food, etc.

5. *I have been counting each animal you counted on. Do you remember how you can do that with your fingers?* (Put the larger number you can't see in your head, show the number you can see with your fingers and bend them down one by one as you count on from the number in your head.) Demonstrate using more problems based on the IP, e.g. there are 4 dragons at another pond and 2 dragons here, 10 frogs under the water and 8 sitting on the stones, …

6. Use the number track to add 2 numbers without referring to the pictures. Ask children put the larger number in their heads and show the second number with their fingers. Ask volunteers to point to the starting number and hop along the number track as children count on and bend down their fingers. Repeat several times, then try without looking at the track.

Pupil activities

SUPPORT ★   Adult-led

You need a 'post box' and a collection of letters. *I post 4 letters* (post them into the box so that they can no longer be seen). *Tom has 2 letters to post. How many letters altogether?* Use a floor number track to show what is happening. Ask one child to jump along to 4 for the letters in the box and then count on 2 more for those to be posted. Retrieve the letters from the post box and count all the letters to check. Record: 4 count on 2 makes 6. Say it together. Repeat with other examples. *Do you need to jump on each number until you get to the starting number?* (no, just listen for the number of letters in the box and stand on that number)

CORE   Adult-supported   IP 3

Give each child a 1–20 number track and a cube to use as a marker. Give examples as in Direct teaching **5**. Children use their track by starting on the hidden number, putting up fingers for the number that can be seen and counting on. Progress to abstract examples, e.g. *What is 6 count on 3? Where do we need to start on the number track? How many do we need to count on? What is the answer?* Ask children to give you a story that matches your example, e.g. *There were 6 shells hidden in the sand and 3 on the top.*

EXTENSION   Independent   AS 25

Children find totals using the counting on method. Have number tracks available for this group to work with if they choose.

Plenary

Key idea: Count on to find a total even if some things are hiding.

1. Invite children who did AS 25 to choose a question to challenge the class. Ask children to choose a method to solve the question and compare answers. Draw pictures on the board to help those who need to see the quantities.

2. Ask children to make up their own examples of 'hidden' numbers problems.

Family activity

● You need a collection of around 20 small objects in a pile. The adult takes a few secretly, and then the child. The adult tells the child how many they have taken and the child counts on their number of objects to find out how many have been taken altogether.

Related play activity

● Set up places to 'hide' a known number of objects, e.g. letters in a post box, cakes in the play oven, dolls in the playhouse. Ask children to make up a problem adding more of the same object to the scene and recording the problem and total in their own way.

Adding and subtracting 6.2 Taking away by counting back

Objectives
● remove a smaller number from a larger number and find how many are left by counting back from the larger number
● begin to relate subtraction to 'taking away'

Key idea	Count back to take away a small number.

Key words   take away, count back

You need   floor number track

Introduction: oral work and mental calculation

Magic number count: Sit children in a large circle. Set a magic number, e.g. 3. Count down from 10 round the circle. When the magic number is reached, the child who says the number stands up. Repeat with the next child starting the count again at 10 till the magic number is reached. When four children are standing up, ask them to sit in the middle of the circle and restart the count round the circle. The next child who says the magic number is the winner.

Main teaching input and pupil activities

Direct teaching

1. Look at the bus queue on IP 7. *How many people are in the queue?* (Count to 10 from the bus stop.) *If 3 people get on the next bus, how many will be left in the queue? Let's take them away.* Cover up the last 3 people. *How many are left?* (1, 2, 3, 4, 5, 6, 7) Remove the cover.

2. *Here's another way to find out.* Count back 3 people from person number 10 to find the answer. Show children 3 fingers to represent the people getting on the bus then all count back from 10 again, bending down 1 finger for each number said … *9, 8, 7. There will be 7 people left. Let's do that together.* Repeat the process, leading children through the counting as you point to each person getting on the bus. Record the number sentence on the board: *10 count back 3 makes 7.*

3. Repeat for other examples, making sure that the number to be counted back is close to the start number as this is when this strategy is most useful.

4. Give children a story problem to solve using this strategy, e.g. *There are 9 plums on the fruit stall. The cat takes 3 of them. How many are left?* Ask a child to solve it by counting back, using fingers and a floor number track to help. Check the answer by covering or crossing out 3 plums on IP 7 and counting the remaining plums. Record a number sentence on the board using 'take away': *9 take away 3 is 6.*

5. Repeat with other examples. Ask children to show each time with number track and fingers how they are counting back to solve the problem.

Pupil activities

SUPPORT ★   Adult-supported

Sing '10 fat sausages', or another rhyme where numbers are taken away. Sing the song again, this time with some of the children as 'sausages'. After each verse up to 5, show what happens, count back from 10 and say a number sentence, e.g. *10 sausages in the pan take away 2 sausages leaves 8 sausages in the pan.* Continue with different numbers in the pan, e.g. *7 sausages in the pan. Take 2 away, how many are left?*

Ask the 'sausages' that are taken away to bend over as you count back: children copy this with their fingers.

CORE   Independent   AS 26

Children use the counting back strategy to solve take away problems with a number track.

EXTENSION   Adult-led

See how children manage if they try to count back mentally: *There are 5 biscuits on a plate.* Ask children to place this first number 'in their head'. *Three get eaten.* Ask children to show how many are going to be 'taken away' on their fingers. They then count back from the first number by bending over one finger for each number counted back till all fingers are bent over. Repeat with children recording each problem as a number sentence, using 'take away', e.g. *5 take away 3 is 2.*

Plenary

Key idea: Count back to take away a small number.

1. Ask the support group to share their work: Choose some of the verses to sing from the song and see if children can show what is happening using their fingers. Ask others to suggest some further verses for the song, e.g. 12 fat sausages, 5 are taken away …

2. Look at work from the core group. Ask individuals to explain how they did one of the questions. Ask everyone to try it by putting the first number in their heads and using their fingers to count back. Ask a volunteer from the support group to move along the number track.

Family activity

- How many are left? Use a collection of up to 10 or 15 objects and an opaque bag. Count some of the objects into the bag. Pull out a few of the objects and count them. Count back to find how many are left in the bag. Check by looking and counting.

Related play activities

- Make 10 fat sausages out of dough and paint. Use to show number sentences in an interactive display.
- Use play people and buses to find out how many are left at the bus stop when some get on.

Adding and subtracting 6.3 How many missing?

Objective	• begin to find how many have been removed by counting up to the larger number

Key idea	**Count up to find how many were taken.**

Key words take away, difference between

You need	two sets of 1–20 number cards (AS 41, 43)
	number track
	purses with five 1p coins and extra 1p coins for Support
	1–6 dice, 7–12 dice for Core pairs
	a 1–6 dice, a 7–12 dice and counters for Extension group

Introduction: oral work and mental calculation

Number card count: Shuffle two sets of number cards and give each child a card. As a class, count forwards from one given number to another (e.g. from 4 to 18). Children hold up their number card when their number is said. Repeat with different number ranges and include counting backwards.

Main teaching input and pupil activities

Direct teaching

1. Use children from the support group to help you in the Direct teaching. Show children a purse containing five 1p coins. *What do you think is in my purse? What coins might there be? Let's look and see.* Take out the coins and show them to the children. Count them one at a time: *1 penny, 2 pence, ..., 5 pence. I have 5 pence.* Give the coins to a child and ask them to check the count.

2. *I am going to ask Richard to take some of my coins without letting anyone see how many.* Look in the purse and count with the children how much is left, e.g. 3p. *I have 3 pence left so how much has Richard got? We know there was 5 pence altogether, so if we count on from my 3 pence until we reach 5 pence, we will find out how much Richard has.* As you count on raise one finger for each number. *I counted on 2, so I think Richard has 2 pence.* Check and see how many Richard has. Show the counting up on a number track and discuss the key idea.

3. Repeat with other examples, altering the initial number of coins. Encourage children to join in with counting on, using their fingers to find out how many have been counted on. Sometimes reinforce the process by showing the same example on the number track. We call the number of fingers the 'difference' between the number we started with and the number we ended with.

4. Use other contexts to find out how much has been taken, e.g. books on a shelf (there were 9, now there are 6). Model number sentences for children to say, e.g. children count up from 6 to 9, keep track of the count with their fingers and say 3. Say together, *6 add 3 is 9; 9 take away 3 is 6. The difference between 9 and 6 is 3.*

Pupil activities

SUPPORT ★   Independent

Children work in pairs. Give each pair a purse with five 1p coins so that they can practise the Direct teaching activity to find out how many coins have been taken from the purse.

CORE   Adult-led

Give pairs of children some items to put in a box. They throw a 7–12 dice to find how many to put in the box and a 1–6 dice to find how many to take out. Demonstrate this in the context of clearing up and putting all the things we don't need in a box to be 'taken away' to the cupboard. Ask children to predict by counting up, how many will be in the box before they take out the items they need. Help pairs to record using pictures and a number track. Use the examples they record to practise saying number sentences together as in Direct teaching **4**.

EXTENSION   Adult-supported

Play 'What's the difference': Use one 1–6 dice and one 7–12 dice. Roll both dice and ask children to identify the smaller number. *How many more are needed to make the larger number?* or *What is the difference between ... and ... ?* Whichever phrasing is used, reinforce the use of the counting on method to find the answer. The game can be played as a small group with each child taking a turn to roll the dice. If they answer correctly they receive a counter. At the end, the child with the most counters is the winner.

Plenary

Key idea: Count up to find how many were taken.

1. Ask children from the support group to show what they were practising. Record each one on a number track for them. Ask children to identify a number sentence each time. *Can anyone tell me another sentence?* Make sure children are using 'difference' correctly.

2. Split the class in half to play a class game of 'What's the difference?'.

Family activity

● Identify situations where things are 'missing', e.g.

Look in the biscuit tin. There were 9 biscuits yesterday. Now there are 6. How many have been eaten?

There are 6 buttons altogether. Two of them are still undone, so how many have you done up?

Related play activity

● Clearing up: Have containers/boxes/trays labelled with how many there should be. How many are missing?

Adding and subtracting 6.4 How many more?

Objectives
- work out by counting how many more are needed to make a larger number
- **SP** choose and use the appropriate number operation to solve 'story' problems involving money
- **SP** explain orally, and where appropriate, record in own way how problem was solved

Key idea	Count up to find how many more.

Key words   difference between, how many more is … than …?, price, cost, pay

You need **AS 27**	purses, 1p, 5p and 10p coins
	a selection of items marked with prices (from 5p to 20p)
	cards with pictures of items and prices (up to 15p)
	0–20 number track (AS 46)

Introduction: oral work and mental calculation

Play 'All change': Say a number. Children start counting forwards from that number. On the command 'change', they start counting backwards from the last number said aloud. On the next command of 'change' children switch to counting forwards. As children gain confidence, vary the starting points and when you call 'change'.

Main teaching input and pupil activities

Direct teaching

1. Give two children a purse each, one containing 7 pennies, the other containing 12 pennies. Ask them to tell the class how much they have and record the amounts on the board. *Can anyone tell me how we can find the difference between the amounts in each purse.* Elicit counting on. *Which number do we start with?* (7) *Why?* (smaller amount). *What number do we need to count on to?* (12) *What do we need to do as we count on?* Elicit using fingers to keep track of how many we have counted on. Count on together. *How many did we count on?* (5) *So what is the difference between 7p and 12p?* (5p) *We can also say 12p is 5p more than 7p.* Repeat for other examples.

2. Have a shop with a selection of items marked with prices from 5p to 20p. *Ross has 10p to spend. What can he buy?* Look at items in shop and say which can be bought and place them together in a group.

3. Pick up something that costs less than 10p. *If Ross pays with a 10p coin, is it fair for the shopkeeper to keep the coin?* Elicit that he needs to give Ross some change to make it fair. Invite a child to be the shopkeeper. *Ross has chosen something that costs 8p and he has paid with a 10p coin. How much more is 10p than 8p?* Ask children for their answers and methods. Show how to work out the difference by counting on. *The difference is 2p. Ross has paid 2p more than it costs. He needs 2p change.* The shopkeeper should give the change by handing over 1p coins as he counts on 2p from 8p. Say together: *8 add 2 is 10.*

4. Repeat with different children coming to the shop to buy one item and other children acting as the shopkeeper who counts on to give the change.

5. *Who can show me something that you cannot buy with 10p?* Group together all the items that cost more than 10p. Pick up one of them, e.g. price 15p. *If I only have 10p, who can tell me how*

much more I need to buy it? Give children time to work this out and ask them to explain how they did it. *Who did the same? Did anyone have a different way?* If counting back was suggested, discuss how both counting on and counting back are good methods (they reach the same answer and you have to do the same amount of counting this time).

Pupil activities

SUPPORT ★ Adult-supported

Continue with the activity in Direct teaching 2.–5. using the items in the shop to find out how much more money is needed or how much change should be given. Change the amounts, e.g. *Sarah has 5p and she wants to buy this ball which costs 8p. How much more does she need?* Encourage children to use their fingers to count and check results by repeating with penny coins.

CORE Adult-led

Play 'Can I buy it?': Use cards with pictures of items and prices. Place these face down in the centre of the circle of children. Give each child a coin, 5p or 10p, or one of each for the more able. Have a 0–20 number track in view. Children take turns to turn over the top card and say the price. *Who has enough money to buy this ...?* ('thumbs up') *Who does not have enough money?* ('thumbs down') Choose a child who does not have enough money to say how much more they would need. Choose one of the children who has enough to say whether they need any change and, if so, how much. Ask children to explain how they worked out the problems: use a number track to check.

EXTENSION Independent AS 27

Write in prices (5p to 20p) on AS 27 before copying it. Tell children they have a 20p coin. Ask them to investigate what they could buy and how much change they would get. Extend to buying 2 items. Children record in their own way.

Plenary

Key idea: Count up to find how many more.

1. Use the items from the shop and different amounts of money to check that children can work out how much more money might be needed or how much change might be given.

2. Pick 2 items that have a different price. *How much more does this cost than that?* Talk about both counting on and counting back. (It's hard to count back more than a few mentally.)

Family activity

- Use shopping items and pennies to ask questions such as:
  This costs 8p. You have only got 5p. How much more do you need?
  This costs 8p. You have paid with a 10p coin. How much change?
  How much more does this cost than that?

Related play activity

- Use 'giving-out' situations where there are 'not enough' of something to work out 'how many more' are needed.

Adding and subtracting 6.5 Coins and change

Objectives
- use coins in role play to give change
- begin to understand and use the vocabulary related to money
- begin to read and write prices such as 8p and £4

Key idea | We can give change in pennies or other coins.

Key words   price, cost, pay, change, altogether

You need   digit cards for all
0–10 number track
| IP 7 | AS 28 | purse, 1p coins, 10p coins
items for class shops with prices less than 10p
selection of coins for Core and Extension

Introduction: oral work and mental calculation

Pose some word problems in a shopping context. Vary the language in the word problems and include both addition and subtraction. Have a 0–10 number track in view.

e.g.   *I bought 1 apple and 4 oranges, how many pieces of fruit did I buy altogether?*
I spent 5p on a banana and 2p on a plum, what was the total cost of the fruit?
I went to the shops with 5p and spent 3p on a sticker, how much did I have left?
I saw a book for 8p but I only had 5p, how much more money did I need?

Children lay out their digit cards in two rows. Wait for 'thinking time' and then ask children to place a finger on card that shows the answer.

Main teaching input and pupil activities

Direct teaching

1. Look at IP 7. *What is the price of the bananas?* (3p each) *... the plums?* (2p each) *... the apples?* (4p each) *... the pears?* (5p each) *What about the oranges?* No price is shown, so agree a price (e.g. 8p) and write it on the IP.

2. *Today we are going shopping. I have some money in my purse for us to spend.* Invite a child to take the coins from the purse. *All the coins are the same: lots of 10p coins. Is there any fruit that costs 10p?* (no) *Does the fruit cost more or less than 10p?* (it all costs less than 10p) *If I give the shopkeeper 10p for one banana would that be fair?* (no) *What will the shopkeeper need to do to make it fair?* Remind children that the shopkeeper will need to give some money back and that this is called 'change'.

3. Remind children how to count on to give change: Act as shopkeeper and choose a child to come with one 10p coin to buy a piece of fruit. Take the 10p. *Now I must count out the change.* Show how to count on from the price up to the 10p that the child has given. Give one penny each time you count. *I have given four 1p coins, so the change is 4p.* Repeat with other children being customers until all the different fruits have been purchased. Then repeat again, each time with children as the shopkeeper and the customers. The rest of the class check that the correct change is given.

4. Develop the activity to children buying 2 items of fruit. *How much do they cost altogether? Do you have enough money? How much change should you get?* or *How much more money do you need?*

Pupil activities

SUPPORT ★ Adult-supported

Set up several small shops using tables in the class. Enact a role-play with children being either customer or shopkeeper. Encourage children to use appropriate language for their role and make sure that all children have a turn at both roles. Give each customer one 10p coin to go shopping with. When the child has made a purchase, they return to the adult with both the item and the change to see how successful they were. *Do you think that the shopkeeper has given you the right amount of change?* To ensure that children are paying with a 10p coin, collect the change and give them another 10p coin. When all items have been bought, the roles of children can be swapped and the shops restocked.

CORE Adult-led

Look at ways of giving change using different coins. Give each pair of children a selection of 1p, 2p and 5p coins and ask them to name the coins. Show children an item priced 7p. *I buy this packet of biscuits for 7p and give the shopkeeper one 10p coin. How much change do I need?* (3p) *The shopkeeper could give me three 1p coins. Can you find another way to make 3p using the coins you have?* Establish that a 2p coin and a 1p coin also make 3p. Repeat with other examples. Each time the children should calculate how much change is needed and which coins could be used. Record different ways of making the same amount of change on a large sheet of paper or the board.

EXTENSION Independent AS 28

Children join in the core activity for one or two examples of using different coins to give change. Give them 20p to spend and ask them to choose from IP 7 what to buy (could be more than 1 item). They choose how to record on AS 28 what they decide to buy, the total cost, what change they should get and what coins could be used to give the change. Have a selection of coins available for children to use if they wish, either to work out the change or to find different ways of making an amount.

Plenary

Key idea: We can give change in pennies or other coins.

1. Ask children who worked on the core activity to act out one of the problems recorded.
2. Develop the above, e.g. *My change is 5p. One coin is 2p. What other coins could I have?*

Family activity

- Practise giving change from 10p (or 20p if appropriate). Label a few items with some prices less than 10p. The adult acts as customer and the child as shopkeeper. Give change using 1p coins or, if appropriate, with a combination of different coins.

Related play activity

- Shopping lists: have a selection of shopping lists. How much change from 10p? Record on list as they buy things in the shop.

Comparing and ordering measures

- *Tell me something in the classroom that is tall, short, long, wide, full, empty, heavy, light, holds a lot, doesn't hold very much at all, ...*

- Ask children to build a tower of bricks. *How many bricks are there in your tower? Compare 3 towers. Whose tower is the tallest? Whose is the shortest? Whose tower fits in between these two?*

- Ask children to build single storey 'factories' with bricks:

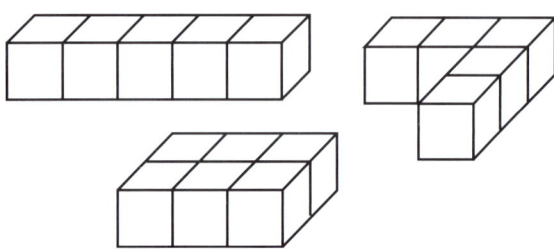

  Whose factory is the longest, the widest, made out of most bricks, ...?

- *Show me something that is longer than this crayon, shorter than this shoelace, taller than teddy, wider than this book, holds more than this matchbox, is heavier than this shoe, ...* Invite children to use direct comparison to check suggestions.

- *Tell me something that is taller/heavier than you, too heavy to pick up, holds more than this cup, ...*

- Order collections of similar items that come in different sizes, e.g. nesting dolls, cereal packets, bottles of drink.

- *Find me something that is the same length as this ribbon, as tall as this doll, as heavy as this book, that holds as much as this carton, ...*

Predicting and estimating

- Show a collection of different sized boxes and some building bricks. Point to a fairly small box. *Do you think some of these bricks will fit in here?* Invite a child to try, counting the bricks as they put them in. Now show a larger box. *Do you think we will get more bricks in this time or not as many?* Invite a child to fill the box with bricks, again counting how many fit in. *Which box holds the most? Can you see a box that you think would hold even more?*

- Show 3 carrier bags: one normal sized, one very small and one very big. Hold up the normal sized bag. *What things in the classroom will fit in this bag?* Repeat with the very small bag and the very large bag. *How many bricks do you think will fit in the smallest bag?*

- Ask children to estimate and then check, e.g. how many cars will fit in a garage ... cups can be filled from a jug ... building bricks will balance a ball ... lolly sticks will fit end to end along a table ... strides to reach the hall.

Time

- *Who can say the days of the week, starting from Monday? Today is Wednesday. What day was it yesterday? What day will it be tomorrow?*

- Use a large analogue clock to read and set o'clock times, e.g. *What time does this clock show? Who can make the clock show 3 o'clock?*

- Read a rhyme or a story including o'clock times. Ask children to read and/or set matching times on a clock face.

Exploring shape

- Show children a 2-D or 3-D shape and ask questions about its properties, e.g. *Is it flat or solid? How many sides/corners has it got?*

- Use a collection of cartons and containers in a variety of familiar 3-D shapes. *What can you tell me about this shape? How is this shape different to this one? What is the name of this shape?*

- Sort same collection of containers. *Can anyone find another container that is the same as this one in some way? How is it the same?* Children may choose non-shape properties such as colour or original contents, so ask questions that focus on shape, e.g. *Can anyone find another container the same shape as this ... has got a square top ... has got a triangle at one end, ...?*

- Play 'Gatekeeper'. Secretly choose a 3-D shape property (e.g. a curved face) or a type of shape without telling the children. Children take turns to choose a shape from a range of 3-D objects and bring it to you. If it matches the criterion, let the child through the gate to stand behind and to one side of you. If the object does not match your criterion, the child stands in front and to the other side of you. Children try to work out which shapes you are letting through. *Who thinks they can pick a shape that I will let in?* Try this activity with flat shapes.

- Display a set of large 2-D shapes. Describe one of the shapes, e.g. *I'm thinking of a shape with 4 sides. All the sides are the same length. All the sides are straight. Who can pick out/tell me the name of this shape?* Try this activity with 3-D shapes.
- Use two identical sets of shapes. Put one set on display and secretly place one shape from the other set in a feely bag. Invite a child to put their hand in the bag and, without removing the shape or pointing to the shapes on display, describe what they can feel. The other children try to guess which shape it is by picking the shape from the set on display or by naming it.
- Use a set of large 2-D shapes. Hide a shape behind a piece of card. Slowly reveal the shape, asking at various stages of uncovering: *What shape do you think this is? Can anyone think of another shape it could be?*

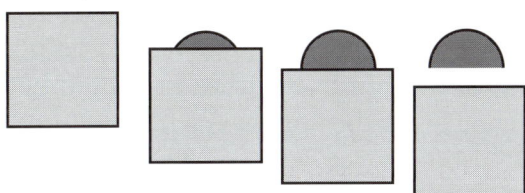

Exploring pattern
- Arrange children in a line. Begin a pattern, e.g. *Stand up, sit down, stand up, sit down, ...; Stand up, sit down, turn around, ...* Children follow the pattern to the end of the line.
- Give each child a few coloured counters. They arrange them in a line of repeating pattern and describe their pattern to others.
- Show a piece of wrapping paper with a simple repeating pattern. Ask children to describe the pattern and then to say the pattern as you move your finger along a row. *What comes next?*
- Thread beads to make repeating patterns.

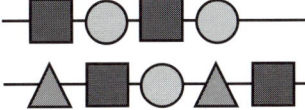

Invite children to continue the patterns and then make/describe their own patterns.
- *Imagine making a pattern of beads (using different colours and/or shapes and/or sizes). Can you describe it? How would it continue?*

- *I made a pattern from squares and circles, but 2 pieces have gone missing:*

 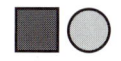

What do you think is missing?

Using pattern to reinforce ordinal numbers
- *Point to the third bead in this pattern:*

What shape is second? Where is the next triangle? Where are the squares?
- *Imagine a red brick, blue brick, red brick, blue brick ... pattern. What colour is the fourth brick? What colour will the sixth brick be?*

Exploring space
- In a large space, give children instructions about position, direction or movement, e.g. *Stand next to ... behind your partner; Turn left and take one step forwards; Take two steps sideways.* Ask individuals to give some instructions.
- When children can follow instructions confidently, play 'Simon says'. If they do not follow an instruction accurately (or react without the 'Simon says' introduction), they sit down. The last child standing is the winner.
- Ask children to describe positions of objects in the classroom. This can include positions relative to other objects, e.g. *The shoe rack is under the coat pegs.*
- Play 'What's my object?' Choose an object in the classroom. Describe where it is, first in general terms (e.g. *It's on a wall.*) then become more specific so children can 'home in' on the item. When they think they know, they can guess your object.
- Give instructions for placing toys relative to each other, e.g. *Put the sheep in the field ... the cow inside the shed ...*
- Give instructions for making a picture: *Put a square on your table. Now put a triangle above the square, pointing up. What have you made?*

Introduction to Comparing and ordering measures: block M3

Vocabulary

- when 2 objects are being compared: *longer, shorter, taller, higher, heavier, lighter*
- when more than 2 objects or measurements are being compared: *longest, shortest, tallest, highest, heaviest, lightest*
- *capacity* is a measure of how much a container will hold

General overview of the topic

Making comparisons is fundamental to measuring. This block introduces the comparison of three measures by direct comparisons of lengths and masses, and by filling and emptying containers.

Children begin to read o'clock times and to be aware of the duration of time.

Comparing and ordering measures 3: Time and comparing more than two measures

Children make direct comparisons of the lengths and heights of groups of three objects. They use the vocabulary 'longer', 'longest', 'shorter', 'shortest', 'taller' and 'tallest' to describe the objects. Children use balance scales to compare directly two objects to find which is 'lighter' or 'heavier'. They then compare a third object with the other two to find the 'lightest' and 'heaviest'. Children compare the capacities of two containers by pouring from one to another and seeing if it holds more or less. They then progress to ordering three containers according to their capacity. Throughout their work on measures, children are encouraged to make predictions about the sizes, weights and capacities of objects.

Children learn to read o'clock times on an analogue clock and carry out practical activities to help them become aware of the duration of time.

Before they start, children need to

- begin to understand and use vocabulary related to comparing measures
- compare directly two lengths, masses or capacities
- begin to understand the vocabulary related to time

Concepts covered next year include

- measuring lengths, masses and capacities using uniform non-standard units
- beginning to measure lengths using standard units
- suggesting suitable units to measure lengths, weights and capacities
- making simple measuring devices
- knowing the seasons of the year
- reading the time to the hour or half hour on analogue clocks

Chief misconceptions

- not lining up one end of each object when comparing lengths
- thinking that, as the object on the 'up' side of a balance is higher than the other object, it must be 'bigger' and therefore heavier

- thinking that if a second container does not get filled when pouring from one container into another, the second container holds less because there is not as much in it
- being misled by the shape of a container when it is part filled, e.g. thinking that because the water level is further up a tall thin container than a wider container, the tall thin one holds more

- confusing the hour hand and minute hand on an analogue clock

Comparing and ordering measures 3.1 Comparing 3 lengths

Objectives
- use language such as longer, longest, shorter, shortest to compare directly 3 lengths
- compare directly 3 lengths
- **SP** make simple estimates and predictions

Key idea	We can compare 3 lengths.

Key words longer, longest, shorter, shortest, taller, tallest, higher, highest, compare

You need

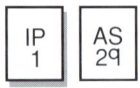

2 books of different length
3 skipping ropes of different length
selection of other objects of different length
card strips
glue
'longer', 'longest', 'shorter', 'shortest' labels

Introduction: oral work and mental calculation

Say a number sequence (counting forwards in 1s, 2s or 10s), asking children to identify a missing number, e.g. 8 in 6, 7, 9, 10.
Repeat with sequences going backwards.

Main teaching input and pupil activities

Direct teaching

1. Show 2 books of different lengths. *How can I find out which of these books is longer?* Reinforce the idea that an end of one book must be in line with an end of the other book.

2. Use 3 skipping ropes of different lengths. Show the shortest one and then the next shortest. *Is this rope longer or shorter than this one?* Ask a child to demonstrate comparing the lengths by laying the ropes one above the other on the ground. Show the third skipping rope. *Do you think this rope will be the longest? How can we find out?* Invite a child to place the rope so that it can be directly compared with other two. Model using the language 'longer', 'longest', 'shorter' and 'shortest' to describe the rope lengths and then ask questions about the ropes that encourage children to use these key words for themselves. Reinforce the vocabulary by writing it on the board.

3. Display IP 1. Focus on groups of 3 similar objects, e.g. houses, towers, flowers, ladybirds, flags. Ask questions about their heights that encourage children to use the vocabulary 'shorter', 'shortest', 'taller', 'tallest', 'higher', 'highest', e.g. *What can you tell me about the height of the house with green windows compared to the house with blue windows?*

4. Investigate the heights of children standing back to back. Invite a child to come and stand at the front. *Who do you think is taller than Bill?* Invite 1 of the suggested children to come out, and compare the heights of the 2 children. *Who do you think is taller than Bronwen?* Invite another child to come out and check to that they are taller. Encourage children to give statements about the relative heights of the children, using the vocabulary 'taller', 'tallest', 'shorter', 'shortest'.

5. Show groups of 3 objects and ask children to predict which is the longest. Invite children to check by direct comparison.

Pupil activities

SUPPORT ★   Adult-supported   AS 29

Show children the cat on AS 29 with a straight card tail added. *Can you make a tail for your cat that is longer than this one?* Children make a tail using a card strip and stick it onto their cat. Ensure they understand that they can make sure their tail is longer by comparing it directly with the original cat's tail. Ask 2 children to show their cats. *Whose cat has the longer tail? Whose cat has the shorter tail?* Choose another child and compare the lengths of the 3 tails. Sort everyone's cats into 2 groups (using 'longer' and 'shorter' labels) by comparing tail lengths with one child's cat: *Who thinks their cat has a longer/shorter tail than Zoe's cat? How can we check?*

CORE   Adult-led

Recap the teaching of comparing the lengths of 3 objects. Invite 3 children to choose an object each from a selection. One child places their object on the floor and the other two use it to compare the lengths of their objects. Ask them to label appropriate objects 'shortest' and 'longest'. Repeat several times, challenging children to predict which object will be longest/shortest. Encourage them to say comparison sentences about the objects.

EXTENSION   Independent

Children work with a partner. They choose 3 objects from a selection each time and compare their lengths. They choose their own method of recording, e.g. drawing pictures one above the other to show relative lengths, drawing pictures labelled 'longest' and 'shortest' appropriately.

Plenary

Key idea: We can compare 3 lengths.

1. Choose 3 children. *Who do you think is the tallest?* Invite the 3 children to come out and stand in a line close together. *Who can say a sentence about how tall Ben is? What about Tyrone? And Ellen?* Repeat with other groups of children.

2. Ask children to compare the heights and lengths of classroom objects, encouraging them to predict first and to make statements using the key words. Focus especially on children who have been working independently.

Family activities

- Child records objects at home that are taller/shorter than them. Recording could be in picture form or in a list with adult scribing.
- Child finds and draws one thing that is shorter than their handspan and one that is longer.

Related play activities

- Challenge children to make a tower taller than themselves using appropriate safe construction materials.
- Children use construction materials to make a long bridge and a shorter one.
- Children find things shorter/longer than their foot.

Comparing and ordering measures 3.2 Comparing 3 masses

Objectives
- use language such as heavier, heaviest, lighter, lightest to compare 3 masses directly
- compare 3 masses directly
- **SP** make simple estimates and predictions

Key idea | We can compare 3 weights.

Key words heavier, heaviest, lighter, lightest, weight, balances, balance scales, compare

You need 0–20 number cards (AS 40, 41, 43)
balance scales
selection of objects of different weight
'heaviest' and 'lightest' labels
puppet
3 parcels of different weight

Introduction: oral work and mental calculation

Show two number cards (e.g. 8 and 14).
Who can tell me a sentence using these numbers and the word smaller? (e.g. 8 is smaller than 14)
Who can tell me a sentence using these numbers and the word larger? (e.g. 14 is larger than 8)
How do we know that 14 is the larger number/8 is the smaller number?
Repeat for several other pairs of numbers.

Main teaching input and pupil activities

Direct teaching

1. Show 2 objects (e.g. a plimsoll and a teddy). *I want to find out which is heavier. What can I use to help me?* (balances/balance scales) Show a set of balances. *How do they work?* Establish that when you put an item in each bucket, the bucket with the heavier item in will be lower.

2. Ask a child to put one of the items into each bucket of the balances. *Who can tell me about the weight of the plimsoll compared to weight of the teddy?* (e.g. The plimsoll is heavier than the teddy.) *Can anyone think of a different way of saying what we found out?* (e.g. The teddy is lighter than the plimsoll.)

3. Show 3 objects. *I want to find out which is the heaviest but that is going to be tricky as I have 3 things and only 2 buckets on my scales. Who can* think how we can use the balances to find out which is the heaviest? Try children's suggestions. Elicit and demonstrate that 2 objects can be compared first and then the heavier one can be compared with the third item.

4. Ask children to attach 'lightest' and 'heaviest' labels to the appropriate objects. Encourage children to say sentences about the relative weights of the objects using the vocabulary 'heavier', 'heaviest', 'lighter' and 'lightest'.

5. Show children another group of 3 objects. *Which do you think is heaviest … lightest?* Invite them to check using balances.

Pupil activities

SUPPORT ★   Independent

Children work in pairs to encourage them to talk about what is happening. They use balances to compare directly the weights of pairs of objects chosen from a selection. Children record their findings by drawing pictures in their books under headings 'heaviest' and 'lightest'.

CORE   Adult-supported

Children work with a partner: each pair needs 2 objects. They predict, and then use balances to find, which object is heavier. Introduce a third object. *How can you find out whether this is heavier than your other 2 objects?* Children compare the weights of the 3 objects (with help where appropriate) and line them up in order, starting with the lightest. They record their findings by drawing their line of objects. Ask each pair to tell the group what they found out, encouraging the use of key vocabulary with questions like: *What did you find out about the yellow car? What can you tell us about the weight of the yellow car compared to the red car?*

EXTENSION   Adult-led

Children work in pairs and choose 3 items from a selection. Challenge them to predict, and then use balances to find, which is lightest. They choose how to record their findings. Discuss with children how they are making their predictions and how they can use balances to compare the weights of 3 objects. Encourage children to describe fully the weight of the middle object, e.g. *It is heavier than the teddy, but lighter than the train. Can you find another object that is heavier than the teddy, but lighter than the train?*

Plenary

Key idea: We can compare 3 weights.

- Use a puppet to talk to children. *I have a problem. Can you help me? I have to find out which of these 3 parcels is heaviest, but my scales have only 2 buckets. What shall I do?* As children explain the method use the puppet to carry out the instructions, making some deliberate mistakes to check children's understanding, especially those who worked independently.
- Once the puppet has found the heaviest parcel it says the method just to check it has got it right. Children show thumbs up for each part it gets right and thumbs down if it goes wrong!

Family activity

- Child predicts which of 3 grocery items is heaviest and which is lightest. If balance scales are available at home, they could check their predictions by comparing directly. They could draw pictures of each item and ask an adult to label the 'heaviest' and 'lightest'.

Related play activities

- Children use balance scales in a shop area to compare the weights of shopping items.
- Challenge children to find items in the shop area that are heavier/lighter than a given object.

Comparing and ordering measures 3.3 Comparing 3 capacities

Objectives
- use language to describe and compare how much 3 containers hold
- compare 3 capacities
- **SP** make simple estimates and predictions

Key idea | We can compare how much 3 containers hold.

Key words holds more/less, holds the most/least, full, empty, container, compare

You need
- 0–20 number track (AS 46)
- selection of suitable containers with different capacities (some numbered for Core activity)
- access to water, sand or rice
- funnels (where needed)
- 'holds more than the jug' and 'holds less than the jug' labels
- 3 different coloured stickers
- 3 plastic 'pop' bottles with different capacities

Introduction: oral work and mental calculation

Ask children to identify hidden numbers on a 0–20 number track and explain how they know, e.g. for 12: *It is the number after 11; It is the number before 13; I got to 12 when I counted along from zero.* Repeat with different hidden numbers, asking children to write each missing number.

Main teaching input and pupil activities

Direct teaching

1. Show children a jug filled with water (or sand or rice) and a few clear containers of different shapes and sizes. *My jug is full. Do you think I can pour all the water into one of these containers?* Ask children to explain their choices, e.g. *The container is taller than the jug.*

2. Invite children to compare the capacity of each container with the jug, by pouring in water from the jug (using a funnel if appropriate). Ensure children understand that if the container holds less than the jug the water will overflow, but if the container holds more than the jug, they will be able to see empty space in the container. Sort the containers into 2 groups labelled 'holds more than the jug' and 'holds less than the jug'.

3. Show 3 containers with different capacities. *Which container do you think holds the most? I am going to start by putting the one I think holds the most here, the one I think holds the least here and the other one in the middle.* Explain your actions as you check whether your predictions are correct. *First I am going to fill the container I think holds the least. Then I'll pour the water into the middle one. What will happen if the middle one does hold more?* (There will be room left for more water.) Demonstrate the pouring. *Does the middle one hold more?* (If it doesn't, adjust the order.) *Now I am going to compare the middle container with the one that I think holds the most. First I need to fill the middle container. Now I am going to pour the water into the third container. What will happen if the third container does hold more?* Demonstrate the pouring and discuss the result.

4. Put coloured stickers on the containers and line them up in order of their capacities. Ask questions to encourage children to use the

vocabulary 'holds more/less' and 'holds the most/least', e.g. *What can you tell me about how much the container with the red sticker holds?*

5. Show 3 different containers. Invite children to predict which holds the most and which the least, and to explain and demonstrate the checking process.

Pupil activities

SUPPORT ★ Adult-led

Children work in pairs. One child predicts whether one container holds more than a second container. The other child checks the prediction by filling one container with water (or sand or rice) and pouring it into the second container. Children use 2 different containers and reverse roles. Encourage children to explain their predictions using appropriate comparative vocabulary, e.g. *This container is wider so I think it will hold more; This container is shorter so I think it will hold less.* You may also wish to guide pairs through a comparison of 3 capacities.

CORE Independent

Children work in small groups and need access to a selection of numbered containers. Each group compares the capacities of 3 containers at a time. Children record results on group table by writing the numbers on the containers under the appropriate headings ('holds least', 'holds more' or 'holds most').

EXTENSION Adult-supported

In pairs children compare the capacities of groups of 3 containers. Encourage children to use the method shown in the direct teaching first and then to go on to explore other methods, e.g. filling the one they think holds most first. Question children to encourage them to describe what they are doing and how they have reached their conclusions.

Plenary
Key idea: We can compare how much 3 containers hold.

1. Show 2 'pop' bottles. *Teddy is at the supermarket and wants to buy the bottle that contains most pop. Which of these 2 bottles do you think he would choose?*

2. *How could we find which is the best choice for teddy?* Choose children who did the support activity to demonstrate comparing the 2 containers.

3. Introduce a third bottle. *Perhaps teddy should buy this bottle instead. How can we find out if it holds more than the other two.* Choose children who worked independently to demonstrate comparing the 3 containers.

4. Discuss any problems children encountered in their activities, e.g. difficulty with prediction, finding it hard to pour without spillage. Children could explain or model successful methods.

Family activity

- Child compares the capacities of containers in the bath to see which holds the most, and talks about their findings with an adult.

Related play activities

- Children order containers in the water/sand tray according to their capacities.
- Children guess and then check how full a container will be when they empty water/sand from a smaller container into it in the water/sand tray.
- Children match cups to toys at a tea party according to their size.

Comparing and ordering measures 3.4 O'clock times

Objectives
- be aware of the language of clock times
- begin to know key times of the day
- begin to read o'clock time

Key idea	When the long hand is at the 12 the time is 'something o'clock'.

Key words clock, hands, o'clock, time

You need individual clocks
large teaching clock

IP 15   AS 30   AS 31

Introduction: oral work and mental calculation

Play some music and ask children to make their fingers dance. Stop the music and say a number no greater than 10. Children show the appropriate number of fingers. Repeat for different numbers. Continue, now asking children to make the numbers in 2 parts, e.g. showing 8 as 4 fingers on one hand, and 4 on the other. (Where children want to show one number greater than 5 they can show the first number then make fist with all fingers, before making the second number.) For each number, try to identify all possible ways.

Main teaching input and pupil activities

Direct teaching

1. Show the large clock. *This is a clock. What can you see on the clock?* Establish that there are numbers and moveable hands, and that one hand is longer than the other.

2. Display IP 15 and point to a 'clock' at the bottom. *I want to make this into a clock. What is missing?* (numbers and hands) *Who can come and write in the clock numbers?* Invite children to fill in the numbers, referring to the teaching clock where necessary. Discuss the numbers, establishing where 1 is and how the numbers to 12 are in sequence around the clock.

3. *What is missing from my clock now?* (hands) *The hands move to show what time it is. I am going to draw the two hands.* Draw hands representing 4 o'clock. *The way I have drawn my hands, the long hand is pointing to the number 12 and the short hand is pointing to the number 4. Where the*

hands are tells me what time it is. Does anyone know what time my clock is showing? Discuss how to read the time. *Whenever the long hand is pointing to the 12, the time will be 'something o'clock'. My little hand is pointing to the 4 so my clock is showing 4 o'clock.* Write 4 o'clock on next to the clock on the IP.

4. *Can anyone think of something they might do at 4 o'clock?* Establish, where appropriate, that 4 o'clock happens twice: once during the day and once very early in the morning. Help children to realise that by 4 o'clock in the afternoon on a school day they will probably have arrived home and might be doing watching TV, eating tea, …

5. Use the large clock to show more o'clock times, asking children to say what the time is. Reinforce that the long hand must points to 12 for an 'o'clock' time but the little hand can point to any number. Encourage children to suggest things that happen at the times made, e.g. school starting at 9 o'clock; lunchtime at 12 o'clock; bedtime at 7 o'clock.

6. Give children individual clocks and ask them to make particular o'clock times. Ask them to explain how they know where to put the hands.

Pupil activities

SUPPORT ★ Adult-led   AS 30

Reinforce how to recognise and read an o'clock time. Make various o'clock times on the large clock and ask children to read them. *Who can make an o'clock time on my clock? Who can read that time?* Children fill in the numbers on the clock face on AS 30 using the large clock for reference. Discuss the arrangement of the numbers with them. Ask children to glue their hands onto their clock to make an o'clock time. *What time have you made?*

CORE   Independent   AS 30

Children fill in the numbers on their clock face and stick on hands to make an o'clock time. They show their clock to a friend, asking them to say what time it is, before recording their time on the AS. Children draw a picture of something they might do at the time they have made.

EXTENSION   Adult-supported   AS 30

Give children individual clocks. Say some o'clock times for them to make. Encourage children to visualise some times by asking, e.g. *If the long hand is on 12 and the short hand is on 3, what time is it?* Children should check using their clocks. They complete the AS by drawing and recording different o'clock times of their choice. *Can I see easily which is the long hand and which is the short hand?*

Plenary

Key idea: When the long hand is at the 12 the time is 'something o'clock'.

1. Ask the class to read the times the core group have made. *Which number are all the long hands pointing to?* Reinforce the key idea.

2. Ask children about o'clock times in the school day, e.g. *What time do we begin school ... have lunch ... go home?* Ask a child to make each time on a clock.

3. Look at the pictures on IP 15 and discuss times at which the events might happen. Record times suggested beneath each picture and ask children to draw hands on a clock face on the IP to show each time.

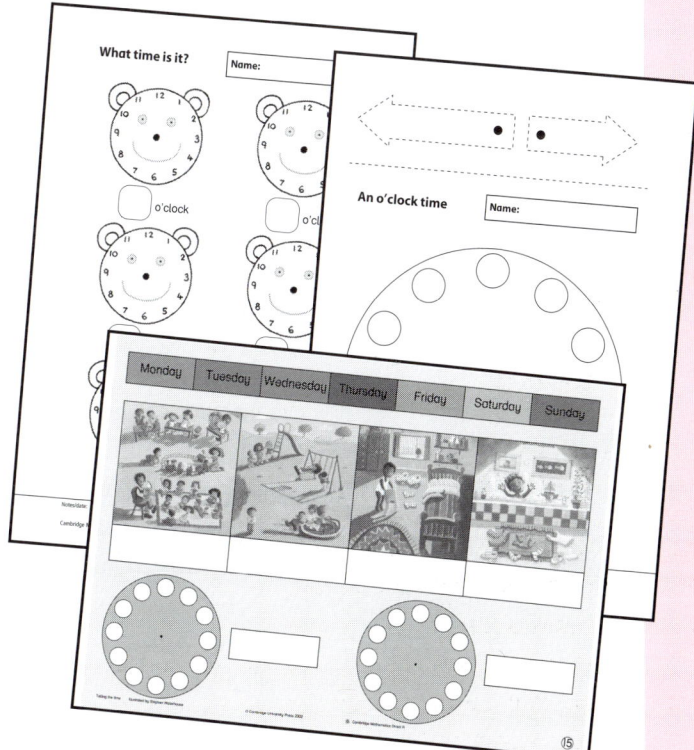

Family activities

● Child spots when a clock at home is saying an o'clock time.
● Child talks to an adult about o'clock times in the family day, e.g. bedtime, tea-time, time to get up, ...

Related play activities

● Children set o'clock times on a clock in the playhouse and act out activities that might happen at that time.
● Children decide times for the class shop to open and close, putting clocks on the shop door to show these times.
● Children play 'What's the time Mr Wolf?'

Comparing and ordering measures 3.5 Time puzzles

Objectives • begin to be aware of the duration of time
• **SP** solve simple problems or puzzles in a practical context

Key idea | Some things take longer than others.

Key words   time, takes longer, takes less time, long/short time, longer/shorter time, timer

You need   counting objects
AS 32 cut into 'cards' and an enlarged copy
1 minute sand timers

AS 32

Introduction: oral work and mental calculation

Tell a story involving adding or subtracting to 10, e.g. *10 teddy bears are playing. If 3 run away and hide, how many are left?* Ask children to use fingers to model what is happening and to show their answer with fingers.

Demonstrate the calculation using counting objects. Repeat for several stories.

Main teaching input and pupil activities

Direct teaching

1. *We are going to think about how long it takes to do different things. Listen while I count to 10 … Think about something you could do that would take less time than my count to 10. Listen again …* Invite children to suggest what they think they could do. Try out some of the suggested activities or alternatives, e.g. buttoning a coat, making a clock say 2 o'clock.

2. *Can you think of anything that would take you longer than my count to 10? What would take even longer? Could you eat an apple … get dressed … write your name?*

3. Suggest a variety of familiar events and discuss whether children think they would take a longer or shorter time than your count to 10, e.g. moving to the carpet, the journey to school, a P.E. lesson, lining up.

4. *Let's make 2 lists, one for things that take a long time and one for things that take a short time.*

Either use a prepared list of activities or take suggestions from children, recording them in the most suitable group.

Pupil activities

SUPPORT ★   Independent   AS 32
Children stick the pictures from AS 32 in 2 groups, under the headings 'long time' and 'short time', according to how long each activity takes. They draw pictures to add some of their own ideas to each group.

CORE   Adult-supported
Show a minute sand timer. *Let's see how long it takes for the sand to go through the timer … Do you think you would be able to write your name before the sand runs out?* Ask children to make predictions. *Whose names will be quicker to write?* (Make the link between the number of letters in a child's name and the time taken to write it.) Start the timer and ask children to see if they can write their name. Repeat for other activities, e.g. writing numbers to 20, drawing 10 circles, …

EXTENSION   Adult-led

Show a minute sand timer. *Let's see how long it takes for the sand to go through the timer.* Explain that you are going to challenge children to write as many number '4's as they can before the sand runs through. *How many do you think you will be able to write?* Start the timer to begin the challenge. Ask children to count a partner's '4's. Record all of the results. *Who wrote the most 4s? What could we try drawing or writing next?* (e.g. the letter h, pictures of flowers) Use suitable suggestions, asking beforehand, e.g. *Do you think you will write/draw more or fewer than before? Why? How many do you think you will be able to write?* Ask children to record one thing they did managed for a group poster with the title 'Before the timer ran out I …'

Plenary

Key idea: Some things take longer than others.

1. Show the enlarged copy of AS 32. Ask children who did the support activity to explain how they decided which activities take a 'long time' and which take a 'short time'. Choose one picture. *Can you see a picture that shows something that would take a longer/shorter time?* Repeat for another picture.

2. Ask children for extra ideas of things that would take a long/short time.

3. Discuss why some activities might take longer for some children than for others (e.g. a child with a long name might take longer to write their name than a child with a shorter name, a child with lace-up shoes might take longer to get dressed than a child with 'slip-on' shoes).

Family activities

- Child draws something at home that takes them a short time to do and something that takes a long time.
- Adult challenges child to do an activity in a given amount of time, e.g. put their toys away before the adult counts to 10.

Related play activities

- Challenge children to do a puzzle before a sand timer runs out.
- Challenge children to build the tallest tower they can before a sand timer runs out.

Introduction to Exploring pattern, shape and space: blocks SS5–6

General overview of the topic

Work on pattern and shape helps children to appreciate that mathematics is all around them. They can easily relate ideas about position, direction and movement to their everyday life and experiences.

Block 5 focuses on recognising and describing properties of 2-D and 3-D shapes and using shapes to create pictures and patterns. Block 6 further develops children's understanding of repeating pattern before settling into its main focus of describing position, direction and movement.

Exploring pattern, shape and space 5: Investigating shapes

Children describe some properties of 2-D and 3-D shapes, applying their knowledge to naming and sorting familiar shapes. They use shapes to make models, pictures and patterns, talking about the shapes they have used and the way the shapes fit together.

Exploring pattern, shape and space 6: Patterns and movement

Children investigate repeating patterns, making predictions about missing elements and how patterns will continue. They use everyday language to describe position, direction and movement and give instructions for others to follow.

Before they start, children need to

- use 2-D shapes to make pictures and patterns
- use 3-D shapes to make models and patterns
- begin to describe the shape and size of solid and flat shapes
- sort and match objects
- begin to name 2-D and 3-D shapes
- begin to use everyday words to describe position, direction and movement

Concepts covered next year include

- extending their knowledge of the names and properties of shapes including the cuboid and cylinder
- making halves of paper shapes by folding them
- beginning to relate 3-D shapes to pictures of them
- making whole and half turns

Chief misconceptions

- confusing the vocabulary used to describe the properties of 2-D and 3-D shapes,
  e.g. referring to the side of a 2-D shape as an edge or the face of a 3-D shape as a side
- believing that there is only one correct way to continue a pattern
  Inviting children to find other possibilities can be enlightening!
- missing out an element of a repeating pattern when the same item starts and ends the unit
  of repeat
  For example, when performing the actions for the repeating pattern: *head, shoulders, knees, toes, head, shoulders, knees, toes, ...* children usually follow the pattern correctly. However, if you change the pattern to: *head, shoulders, knees, head, head, shoulders, knees, head, ...* where *head* starts and ends the repeating unit, children often miss one of the *heads*.

Exploring pattern, shape and space 5.1 Sorting solid shapes

Objectives
- understand and use in practical contexts words to describe flat and solid shapes
- **SP** begin to name, match and sort shapes

Key idea	When we describe a solid shape we talk about its faces, corners and edges.

Key words   shape, flat, curved, straight, solid, hollow, corner, face, side, edge, end, cube, pyramid, cone, sphere

You need   a cube, pyramid, cone and sphere labelled in a class display

 IP 10

a feely bag

sets of 3-D shapes: cube, pyramid, cone, sphere

shapes for children to build with

Introduction: oral work and mental calculation

10 children stand in line and raise a hand in turn as the class counts to 10, lowering it on the count back to zero. Extend to counting to 20 with children raising both hands.

Sing a counting rhyme, e.g. 'One, two' from *Seven Dizzy Dragons*, Cambridge University Press 1997. Children show their fingers or clap as they count.

Main teaching input and pupil activities

Direct teaching

1. Show children the 3-D shapes and say the name of each shape with children repeating it. Place the shapes where all children can see them.

2. Look at IP 10 together. *Who can point to a cube, ... a cone, ... ?* Ask children to pick up and match the solid shape to its representation each time.

3. *We are going to learn some new words to help us describe the different solid shapes.* Hold up a cube and ask for its name. Point to one face. *This flat part of the shape is called a 'face'. Who can point to another face on the cube?* Repeat for all faces. *Are all the faces on this shape the same or different?* (same) *What shape is each face?* (square) *Is the face curved or flat?* (flat) Ask children to show their hand in a flat position, then to make it curved.

4. Show the sphere. *Does this shape have a flat face?* Roll it in front of the children. *It has a curved face and I can roll it like a ball. Who can pick up a different shape with a curved face?* (cone) Encourage children to use flat and curved hands to help them identify if faces are flat or curved: name the flat faces. *Will this shape roll?* Ask a child to demonstrate.

5. Point to the edge on the cone. *This is called an 'edge': it is where the flat face and the curved face meet or join.* Ask children to say the word. Look at other shapes and identify edges. *Are all the edges straight?* (No, some are curved)

6. Show a pyramid. Point to a corner. *This is where all the edges meet and we call it the 'corner'. Who can find another corner on this shape?* Invite children to come and point to corners. Look at other shapes and identify corners.

7. *I want to make a set of shapes that all have flat faces. Who can find a shape for my set?* Invite children to put shapes into the group. Make other sets, e.g. shapes with 1 flat face, shapes with more than 1 corner, ...

Pupil activities

SUPPORT ★ Adult-supported

Go over the names of the solid shapes. Without children seeing, place one shape in a feely bag. Pass the bag round the group: ask children to feel it and say one thing about the shape. Prompt where necessary by asking questions, e.g. *Can you feel any corners? Does it have any edges? What do the faces feel like?* When all children have had a turn summarise what they said. *Can anyone tell me the name of the shape?* Repeat, encouraging children to use 'face', 'edge' and 'corner'. Model correct language as needed.

CORE Adult-led

Go over the names of the solid shapes together. Give each child a shape and ask them to name it. Write a label: shapes with a square face □. *Who has a shape that can go in this set?* Ask children who still have a shape to hold it up and check none have square faces. Repeat for different sets. Can children suggest a set to make?

EXTENSION Independent

Children work in pairs, facing each other with a book standing in between. Child A chooses a shape secretly and places it so that child B cannot see it behind the book. Child A then tells child B 3 things about the shape. Child B tries to guess the shape. Children agree on what shape it is, referring to a class display if unsure. Repeat, swapping roles each time, until the end of the activity time.

Plenary

Key idea: When we describe a solid shape we talk about its faces, corners and edges.

1. Play 'I-spy shapes', e.g. *I spy with my little eye something with 4 corners, something shaped like a cone/cube/sphere, …*

2. *What is my shape? I am thinking of a shape with … straight edges … a round end … corners … flat faces.* Elicit suggestions, asking children to explain why some guesses are incorrect. Repeat for other shapes. When a guess is correct, show children and reinforce the properties of the shape.

3. Discuss any problems or misconceptions, e.g. confusing edges and corners. Can anyone think of a way of remembering? Remind children that hollow spheres, cubes, etc. have the same names as solid shapes.

Family activity

● Play 'I-spy shapes': *I spy with my little eye something with 4 corners, …*
shaped like a cube, …

Related play activity

● Build models with 3-D shapes.

Exploring pattern, shape and space 5.2 Copying models

Objective • use 3-D shapes to make models, pictures and patterns

Key idea Shape and space words help us describe how to make a model.

Key words shape, flat, curved, straight, solid, hollow, corner, face, side, edge, end, cube, pyramid, cone, sphere

You need cubes, cones, pyramids, spheres (as many of each of a similar size as possible)
cards with picture and names of the 3-D shapes

Introduction: oral work and mental calculation

I'm thinking of a shape. What could it be? Draw part of the shape on the board and elicit suggestions. Add to the shape until it is complete.

Say a counting rhyme, e.g. 'Ten little teddies' from *Seven Dizzy Dragons*, Cambridge University Press 1997.

Main teaching input and pupil activities

Direct teaching

1. Remind children of the names of the shapes and match them to the picture cards.

2. Use 3-D shapes to build a simple model. As you place each shape, ask children to name it and talk about its properties, e.g. *Tell me about the faces. Does it have flat or curved edges? Does it have any corners?* Vary questions asked for each shape to reinforce its main properties.

3. Invite a child to come and copy the model. Ask other children to help give instructions, i.e. name the shapes and describe where they must go. Encourage children to use space (positional) words, e.g. on top of, next to, behind, in front of, between. If the child is confused by an instruction ask others if they can say it in a different way. Discuss how some instructions are not clear. Highlight good use of vocabulary, modelling the use of unfamiliar words.

4. Keep your original model but reuse the children's copy. Repeat **2.** and **3.** for another model(s). Involve more children by asking each to place one shape. Focus on the language of instructions. To extend some children tell them which shape to place by referring to its name or properties. Keep the original model each time.

Pupil activities

SUPPORT ★ Independent

Using a selection of reclaimed 3-D shapes children build their own model, copying the model(s) already built.

CORE Adult-supported

Children work in pairs. They sit facing each other with a barrier between them, e.g. large book. Child A quickly builds a model with four 3-D shapes. Child A then tells child B how to build the same model. When the copy is complete, children compare models and then swap roles. Model the process first and then guide pairs in how they can make their instructions clearer. Look out for any misconceptions/incorrect use of language.

EXTENSION   Adult-led

Make repeating patterns with 3-D shapes, e.g. cube, sphere, cube, sphere... Ask children to describe the pattern by naming the shapes correctly. *What will be the next 3 shapes in the pattern? How many different patterns can we make using just cubes and spheres?* Investigate together, e.g. c c c s s s c c c s s s;

    c c s c c s c c s c c s

Ask children to work in pairs, one child using 2 different 3-D shapes to create a pattern for their partner to copy, and then swapping roles.

Plenary

Key idea: Shape and space words help us describe how to make a model.

1. Look at models made by the support group. Ask children to identify the shapes they used: *Who can name this shape? Who can point to a cube? How many of each shape have been used? Which model has the most shapes?*

2. Discuss Core activity. Identify common problems, e.g. using positional language. Reinforce by asking children to describe the position of an object in the classroom.

Family activity

- Go on a 'shape hunt' at home. Look for things that are cones, spheres, pyramids or cubes. Draw them or ask an adult to make a list for you.

Related play activity

- Build models using reclaimed 3-D shapes.

Exploring pattern, shape and space 5.3 Sorting flat shapes

Objectives ● begin to name and sort 2-D shapes
● **SP** respond to a given criterion for sorting, then suggest own criterion

Key idea	We can sort flat shapes.

Key words shape, flat, curved, straight, corner, side, circle, triangle, square, rectangle, star

You need feely bag with a cone, cube, pyramid, sphere
sets of 2-D shape templates (rectangles, squares, triangles, circles,
IP 10   AS 33   stars for Direct teaching: more for Extension)
labels

Introduction: oral work and mental calculation

Put some 3-D shapes in a feely bag and pass it round. Encourage children to hold one inside the bag and describe it, e.g. all the faces on my shape are flat, one of the faces is a square, ... Other children guess what it might be.

Take out the shapes. Ask children to find solid shapes around the classroom that match each one. Talk about the shapes of all the flat faces on the solids, noting which children know the names.

Main teaching input and pupil activities

Direct teaching

1. *We are going to look at flat shapes and see how we can sort them into different sets.* Show different flat shapes and remind children of their names. Look at IP 10. *Who can point to a square?* Look at the star and ask children to describe it.

2. Show children a selection of different rectangles, including squares. *Who can tell me what is the same about all these shapes?* Elicit or demonstrate that they all have 4 sides. *I want to sort these shapes into 2 sets, one set of squares and one set of shapes with 4 sides that are not squares.* Put out 2 set circles and place a square at the edge of one and a 'not-square' at the other (the word 'oblong' is not introduced until year 4). Hold up several of the shapes in turn identifying each one as square or not-square. Hold up a further shape and ask children to identify it. *How do you know it is a square or not a square?* Elicit that a

square has 4 straight sides all the same length. Invite children to come and place the shapes in a set. When all shapes have been correctly sorted reinforce the properties of squares and not-squares.

3. Repeat for a selection of different types of triangles and stars. *Now we are going to sort these shapes into 2 sets. What 2 sets could I make?* (triangles and not triangles) Invite a child to 'label' each set circle with a shape. *How do we know if a shape is a triangle?* Elicit that a triangle has 3 straight sides and 3 corners. *Does anyone know what the other shapes are called?* (stars) Elicit that a star has straight sides and 'outside corners' (points) and 'inside corners'. Invite children to come and place each shape in a set. Reinforce the properties of triangle and star.

4. Show a selection of squares, rectangles, triangles, circles and stars. *Let's sort these shapes into 2 sets, one set of shapes with straight sides and one set of shapes with curved sides.* Place labels with '−' and ')' on set circles. Invite children to come and place shapes in the

correct set. *What do you notice about the shapes in the set with curved sides?* (they are all circles) Remind children that a circle has one curved side.

5. You could ask children to find another way of sorting the shapes.

Pupil activities

SUPPORT ★ **Adult-led** IP 10

Ask children to find a flat shape on IP 10, name it and pick out a matching shape. If an incorrect shape is selected, ask other children to help by talking about the properties of the shape. Sort shapes by properties, e.g. shapes with more than 3 corners and shapes with 3 or less corners, shapes with all sides the same length and shapes with sides of different lengths, shapes with more than 3 sides and shapes with 3 sides or less, ... As children place shapes in sets ask them to say why they chose that set. Highlight good language and model correct use as needed.

CORE **Independent** AS 33

Children sort shapes by colouring the same shapes with the same colour.

EXTENSION **Adult-supported**

Give children large sheets of paper with a set title at top, e.g. shapes with 4 sides, shapes with no corners. Children draw round thin card or plastic shapes to create a set matching the heading. They can then choose their own heading. The sheets can be put together later to make a book. Ask children why they have chosen each shape and make suggestions for shapes they have not included in their set.

Plenary

Key idea: We can sort flat shapes.

1. Use IP 10. Ask children to name the shapes they can see (flat or solid). Invite them to put a cross on each shape till all are identified.

2. Wipe off the crosses and ask children to a find shape to fit given criteria, e.g. *Who can find a shape that has ... 3 sides and 3 corners? ... 6 points? ... curved sides? ...* When the shape has been found ask children to name it.

Family activity

● 'Collect' road signs on walks or car journeys. The person who collects the most, e.g. triangles or circles wins.

Related play activity

● Print with solid shapes to see which flat shapes can be made, or print with potatoes cut with different shapes.

Exploring pattern, shape and space 5.4 Drawing 2-D shapes

Objectives
- begin to name 2-D shapes
- use 2-D shapes to make pictures and patterns
- begin to sketch 2-D shapes

Key idea	'See' a flat shape in your head before you draw it.

Key words shape, flat, curved, straight, corner, face, side, circle, triangle, square, rectangle, star

You need	sets of 2-D shapes
	large rectangle drawn on paper or board
	individual whiteboards or pencil and paper

Introduction: oral work and mental calculation

Show me a …circle, square, triangle, rectangle. Children can make the shape with their fingers, hold up a shape template or show a face from a solid shape.

Sing 'Imaginary pictures' from *Seven Dizzy Dragons*, Cambridge University Press 1997, if available.

Main teaching input and pupil activities

Direct teaching

1. *We are going to learn how to draw flat shapes.* Hold up shapes and check that children know their names.

2. Briefly show children the large rectangle and then hide it. Ask children to close their eyes and see if they can 'see' the shape in their minds. They should keep eyes closed and nod or shake head as appropriate in answer to questions, e.g. *Can you see how many sides it has? Can you see how long the sides are? Can you see if the sides are straight or curved? Can you see if there are any corners? What shape can you see?* Show the drawing briefly again, hide it and give children time to draw it. *Which part of the rectangle did you draw first? Which part was tricky?* Take feedback and then model drawing a rectangle: focus on its properties as you draw.

3. *Let's look at a different shape. Think about the things that will help you to draw it. Are the sides straight or curved? How many sides/corners does it have? Which way do the corners point?* Repeat step 2 for a circle, square and triangle.

4. *Can you think of a shape we have not drawn?* Elicit 'star'. *Here's a quick way to draw a star with 6 points.* Model the method of drawing a star by drawing one triangle and then another upside down. Show children how they can turn their books or paper to help draw a triangle upside down or to use dots for the corners of the second triangle and then join these. Give children a chance to try this out.

5. Draw 2 linked shapes. Use the process in **2.** to see if children can draw them from memory.

Pupil activities

SUPPORT ★   Adult-supported

Ask children to create a picture by drawing round shapes. They should make the picture first, e.g. person, train, ship, flower, house, … and then draw round the shapes. Show children how to hold shapes still with one hand so they can draw round accurately with the other. They could also use what they have learnt from Direct teaching to add smaller shapes drawn in by hand. Check that children can name all the shapes in their picture and tell you how many of each shape have they used.

CORE   Adult-led

Ask children to draw a square: reinforce its properties as they draw.

Can you draw another square that is bigger? Discuss different strategies children used. *How do you know it is bigger?* (e.g. 'the smaller square is inside the larger one' or 'all the sides are longer')

Ask children to draw a rectangle. *Can you draw another rectangle that has the short sides in a different position?* Show children how to turn (rotate) a rectangle.

Show children how to change a shape into a drawing, e.g. a circle can become a face, a plate with food on, a wheel on a car, a clock. Ask children to suggest other ideas and each try one out. Repeat for other shapes. If children record pictures on separate pieces of paper you can put these together to make a book 'What shape am I?'.

EXTENSION   Independent

Challenge children to draw one of each of the flat shapes they have looked at. Can they draw a bigger/smaller one?

Plenary

Key idea: 'See' a flat shape in your head before you draw it.

1. *What shapes can you see in the classroom? Which of the shapes is hard to draw? Why?* Discuss ways of making it easier. *Which is easy? Why?*

2. Use individual white boards or paper and pencils. *Draw a big circle, ... a small triangle, ... a square, ... a rectangle smaller than the square, ...*

Family activity

- Make shape biscuits, either real or pretend, e.g. squares, triangles, circles. Talk about the number of corners and sides.

Related play activity

- Draw round shapes to make 2-D shape pictures.

Exploring pattern, shape and space 5.5 Pictures and patterns from flat shapes

Objectives
- use 2-D shapes to make pictures and patterns
- talk about, recognise and create patterns
- talk about the shapes that have been used in the patterns and how they fit together

Key idea We can use flat shapes to make pictures and patterns.

Key words shape, pattern, corner, side, circle, triangle, square, rectangle, star

You need 2-D shape templates
felt shapes
gummed shapes

IP 11 AS 34 AS 35

Introduction: oral work and mental calculation

Choose a shape (flat or solid) and encourage children to talk about it, e.g. *Is it flat or solid? What can you tell me about its sides?* Introduce a second shape and ask children to say what is different about it, e.g. that shape has 3 sides; this shape has 4 sides; that shape is solid and this shape is flat; ...

Main teaching input and pupil activities

Direct teaching

1. *We are going to use flat shapes to make pictures. What shapes could we use?* Go over names of flat shapes and match to shapes on IP 11.

2. Model making a picture of a house using 2-D shapes. Ask children to name shapes they can see in the picture. As you draw ask questions, e.g. *How many sides do I need in my square? What is special about the sides of a square? How many corners are there in my triangle? What other shape could I use for the chimney?* Highlight the properties of the shapes and use of correct vocabulary.

3. *We can also use shapes to make patterns.* Look at IP 11. *Who can see a pattern of shapes in the picture?* Invite children to come and point to patterns in the picture, e.g. on scarves, trousers and dress on washing line, along each border, ... *I am going to make a pattern on the caterpillar: can you tell me what it is as I draw it?* Create a repeating pattern with 2 shapes,

e.g. O ☐ O ☐ O ☐
Who can tell me the next shape in the pattern? Repeat for other patterns.

4. *I am going to make a pattern in the circles at the bottom of the picture. Think about what comes next?* Draw shapes in a repeating pattern in the circles. *Who can come and draw in the next shape?* Ask children to describe the pattern. Repeat for other patterns of increasing complexity.

Pupil activities

SUPPORT ★ Adult-supported AS 34
Use felt shapes to make a picture.
Which shapes have you used? How many triangles, ...?
Help children to make a simple repeating pattern in the border.

CORE Independent AS 34
Ask children to draw round 2-D shape templates or 3-D shapes to make a picture. They can also create a simple repeating pattern in the border.

EXTENSION   Adult-supported   AS 35
Use IP 11. Look at the vertical repeating patterns on scarves and in the border. Discuss which way the patterns go. Use shapes to create a vertical repeating pattern: *Who can describe this pattern? What would the next 3 shapes be?* Decide together whether the colour of each shape matters. Invite a child to come and continue the pattern. Repeat for other patterns. Ask children to use gummed shapes to make repeating patterns on the hat and scarf on AS 35.

Plenary
Key idea: We can use 2-D shapes to make pictures and patterns.

1. Discuss picture-making. *Which shapes ... fit together exactly? ... have spaces round them?* Ask the support group to describe their pictures.
2. Discuss any problems children encountered, e.g. in fitting shapes together, in making a repeating pattern, ...
3. Ask the Extension group to show and describe their scarf patterns.

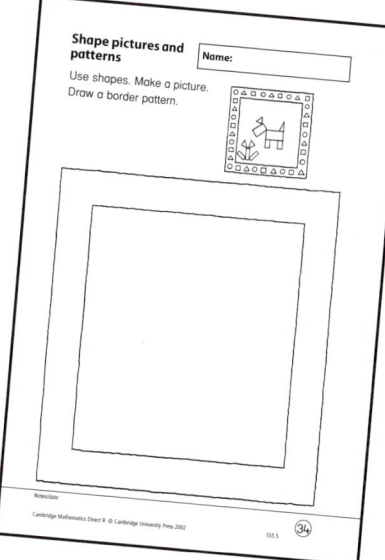

Family activity
- Use sticky or felt shapes or shapes from AS 35 to make pictures and talk about the shapes used.

Related play activities
- Make shape pictures using flat shapes.
- Make necklaces with repeating shape patterns.

Exploring pattern, shape and space 6.1 Repeating patterns

Objectives
- talk about, recognise and create patterns
- **SP** make simple estimates or predictions

Key idea | Say and repeat the pattern to find the missing parts.

Key words | repeating pattern

You need | cubes
IP 11 | AS 36 | counters of 2 sizes
plastic teddies
shapes of different colours and size (circles and triangles for Support)

Introduction: oral work and mental calculation

Your finger is a magic pencil. Use your magic pencil to draw a circle, ... a triangle, ... a big square, ... a smaller square, ... a little rectangle, ...

Read 'Imaginary pictures' from *Seven Dizzy Dragons*, Cambridge University Press 1997 while children perform the actions.

Main teaching input and pupil activities

Direct teaching

1. Look at IP 11. *Who can see some patterns?* Invite children to describe patterns they can see. Indicate the pattern in the right hand border of the picture: circle, triangle, rectangle. *We call this a repeating pattern.* Ask a child to describe it. *Let's find the next shape in the pattern.* Point to each shape and say the names together indicating the next (imaginary) shape as children say triangle. *How do we know the next shape is a triangle?* (it comes after the circle each time, the pattern repeats, ...)

2. *Can you see any other repeating patterns in the picture?* Scarves on washing line and pattern in left border. Ask children to describe the patterns and to say what would come next.

3. *I am going to make another repeating pattern in the circles.* (Colour circles red, red, blue, blue, green, green, red, red.) Ask children to describe the pattern. *We can continue the pattern. Who can colour in the next 2 circles?* Invite children to come and colour in remaining circles. Ask other children to predict which colour is going to be used and how they know.

4. Rub out some of the parts of the pattern. *Now there are some parts missing. How can we find out what the missing parts are?* (Say the repeating pattern and match to the missing parts.) Invite children to come and replace the missing parts of the pattern. Check by saying the pattern from the beginning. *Do we need to go right back to the beginning each time we check the pattern?* Encourage children to explain what they think.

5. Repeat with different patterns both on IP 11 and on the floor using cubes, counters, shapes, numbers, colours, teddies of different sizes, ... Be careful to vary only one property, e.g. size, shape or colour. Show children patterns that are vertical as well as horizontal.

Pupil activities

SUPPORT ★ Independent AS 36
Children use triangles and 2 sizes of circle to copy patterns on AS 36, and fill in the missing shape. They then draw the missing shape in the box. They can then make their own repeating patterns and draw round the shapes to record them.

CORE   Adult-supported

Use cubes to make a repeating colour pattern with some gaps. Ask children to describe the pattern of colours. Invite individuals to come and fill the gaps. Encourage them to explain how they know which colours are missing. Repeat with other patterns, then ask children to work similarly in pairs: Child A secretly makes a pattern with some parts missing; Child B fills in missing parts. Swap roles. Check children are making patterns that repeat, and that missing parts have been correctly filled in. Ask children to describe their patterns and how they worked out the missing parts.

EXTENSION   Adult-led

Develop main teaching by introducing patterns that have more than one variable, e.g. size and colour. Make a pattern and ask children to describe it, e.g.

Repeat with a different pattern. *What will come next?* With the next pattern leave some gaps and ask children to identify missing parts. Give them 2 sizes of counter in varied colours. Ask them to make their own patterns in pairs: child A secretly makes a pattern with some parts missing; child B fills in missing parts. Swap roles.

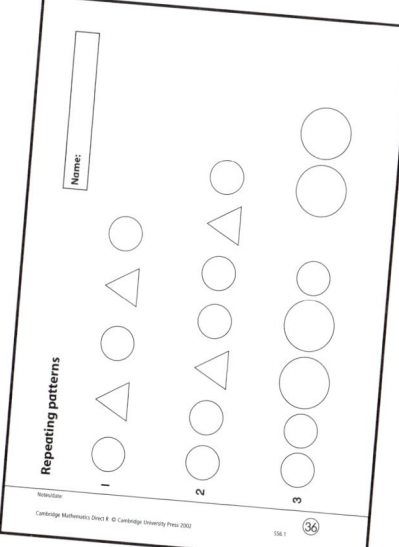

Plenary

Key idea: Say and repeat the pattern to find the missing parts.

1. Draw some repeating patterns on the board, leaving gaps. Use a puppet and tell children that the puppet has made some patterns but has missed some parts out. *Can we help him find what's missing?* Invite children from the support group to suggest ways of explaining the process to the puppet and help him find missing parts in the repeating patterns.
2. Discuss any problems and misconceptions. *Has anyone got a different way?*
3. Remind children that they have been looking at 'repeating patterns' that can go on and on.

Family activity

- Make your own repeating pattern. Use different colours or shapes. Can you make your pattern into a headband for your teddy or doll?

Related play activity

- Make repeating patterns by printing with potatoes or shaped sponges.

Exploring pattern, shape and space 6.2 Describing position

Objective	● use everyday words to describe position

Key idea	There are lots of words to describe where something is.

Key words	behind, in front of, next to, beside, opposite, in(side), outside, on (top of), under(neath), over, between, above, below, before, after, close, far

You need

IP 16 AS 37

car mat and cars or a farm model and animals
feely bag
a large book
farm/zoo animals
teddy or similar toy

Introduction: oral work and mental calculation

Children sit in a circle. One child starts the count from zero and it passes round the circle in a clockwise direction. When 10 is reached that child stands up and the count continues round the circle, this time counting back to zero, when that child stands up. Talk about the number pattern that children are making.

Main teaching input and pupil activities

Direct teaching

1. Introduce IP 16. *Let's talk about where the animals are in the zoo … When we talk about where things are we say we are talking about their positions.* Give some examples from the classroom using vocabulary children have met before, e.g. *My position is* **on** *the chair. Peter's position is* **next to** *Jeevan. The tiger in the picture is* **under** *the table.*

2. Ask children questions that require them to look at the positions of animals and objects on IP 16. Encourage children to use positional vocabulary (key words) to answer, introducing and demonstrating any that are unfamiliar, e.g. *Where is the monkey?* (on the branch) *Where is the baby elephant?* (behind the mummy/daddy) *Where is the red ball?* (on the sea-lion's nose) *Where is the zoo-keeper?* (outside the tiger's cage) *What is on top of the tiger's cage?* (a bird) *What is between the monkeys?* (a hat) *Which animal is above the sea-lion?* (monkey) *Which animal is below the tiger?* (elephant) Write some of the common or simpler words on IP 16 as you use them, e.g. on, under, in, between, next to, …

3. Use some farm or zoo animals, a book, a feely bag and some children. Ask individuals to come out and put the items or themselves in the position you describe, e.g. *Put a cube inside the feely bag. Stand opposite me. Put the book between 2 animals. Make a line of animals: put the sheep before the cow and the pig after the cow.* Reinforce the correct use of the key words and rectify any misconceptions.

Pupil activities

SUPPORT ★ Adult-supported

Work with a farm model or car mat. Use the more common key words to ask individuals to place different items in different positions. Each time they should say where they have put each one. Help children to take turns around the group to give instructions to another child in the same way.

CORE   Adult-led

Use a teddy bear or other animal and some objects from the classroom, e.g. chair, empty box. Give children instructions using positional language and see how accurately they can follow. *Paul can you put the teddy between Sarah and Jake? Where is the teddy? John can you put the teddy under the box? Emily can you put the teddy on the chair? Elena can you put the teddy beside Toby?* Invite individuals to come and put teddy in a different position. *Where is teddy now? Who can put teddy is a different place?* Repeat with children saying where teddy is each time and model correct language where needed.

Ask children to draw a picture to show the position words 'under' and 'over'. Scribe a sentence for children using these words.

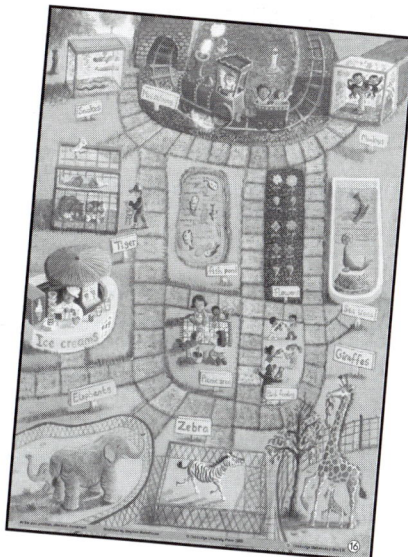

EXTENSION   Independent   IP 16   AS 37

Children follow instructions relating to position and complete the picture. Have IP 16 with position words in view. Then work in pairs and give instructions to make a drawing together.

Plenary

Key idea: There are lots of words to describe where something is.

1. Play 'I spy' position game: *I spy with my little eye something that is on the table.* Children then guess the item by looking to see what is in that position. Repeat using different positional language.

2. Ask the extension group to explain their activity and show their work.

3. Discuss any problems or misconceptions. *Can anyone help?*

Family activity

● Play 'I spy' position game with another person: *I spy with my little eye something that is on the table. Look at the table. What is there?* Repeat using different positional language.

Related play activity

● Paint a picture with creatures in different positions.

Exploring pattern, shape and space 6.3   Describing direction

Objectives
- use everyday words to describe direction
- listen to and discuss stories

Key idea | **We can describe which way to go.**

Key words   direction, left, right, up, down, across, along, around, through, to, from, towards, away from

You need   blank cards

Pat Hutchins, *Rosie's Walk*, Red Fox 2001
toys/construction sets/modelling materials for Rosie's walk
a small model person

Introduction: oral work and mental calculation

Ask 10 children to line up and all sing '10 green bottles'. Children sit down when they 'fall off' the wall.

Main teaching input and pupil activities

Direct teaching

1. *We are going to look at how we can say which way to go or what 'direction' to go in.* Introduce *Rosie's Walk* by Pat Hutchins. *Who do you think Rosie is? Where do you think she is going on her walk?* Read the story. Invite children to join in with hand actions to show where she goes. *Who can remember which is their left hand?* (hold up hands as if surrendering: the thumb and forefinger of the left hand forms an 'L')

2. Look at the pictures in the book again. *Where is Rosie going? Let's see if we can find lots of ways to describe which direction Rosie is going in.* Help children to find alternative ways, e.g. for 'around the pond' could say 'along the edge of the pond', 'next to the pond', 'past the tree'. Reinforce that we can use different words and phrases to communicate the same instruction. Use a card to write and show each word as it is used and draw a visual clue related to the story next to it. Encourage children to use vocabulary carefully and to name objects correctly to add clarity to the description, e.g. 'she is going over there'

would be better as 'she is going towards the tree with the nest in it'.

3. Look at the book again: this time describe where the fox goes. *Is it exactly the same as Rosie? What parts are different?*

4. Introduce the idea of making one big picture of Rosie's walk. *I want to put in all the things she saw and to show the way that she walked. Where did Rosie start her walk? Where did she go next? What things did Rosie see?* Make a large picture map of the walk, drawing the things she saw in appropriate places. As children describe the walk show the route Rosie took on the picture. Encourage them to use vocabulary clearly and accurately.

Pupil activities

SUPPORT ★   Adult-supported

Go for a walk around school. Ask children to remember which places they pass and how they go. Think about going around, under, over, across, behind, in front of, right and left. Stop frequently and ask children to describe what they have just done, e.g. we walked across the hall, we went behind the shed, we went down the steps. Make a group book of 'Our walk around school': ask each child to illustrate a different part of the walk and then to give a sentence to match the picture. Help children to sequence the pictures in the order they happened.

CORE   Independent

Make a model based on Rosie's walk using construction or play equipment. Give children the book and word cards made in Direct teaching **2.** to help them include a variety of directional words. Ask them to place the cards to show the way Rosie went.

EXTENSION   Adult-led   IP 16

Look at IP 16. *What animals can you see?* Place a model person by the tigers. *What if I am standing by the tigers, but I want to go to the monkeys? Who can draw on which way to go?* Look at the route. *Who can tell me how to get there?* Take several descriptions encouraging a wide use of the key words and reference to other objects in the picture. *Has anyone got a different way to draw on the picture* Take descriptions of the route. Repeat for other starting points and destinations chosen by children.. Ask children to choose one animal to visit and to draw the route showing things they would pass on the way. They need to show where they are starting. Observe what approach children take and how clearly they can record the route.

Plenary

Key idea: We can describe which way to go.

1. Ask children from the core group to show and describe their model of Rosie's walk. Encourage the use of directional language, e.g. left, right, up, down, across, around, under, ...

2. Look at IP 16. Invite children from extension group to explain how they were finding ways to go from one animal to another. *I am going to give you some directions and I want to see if you can find out the animal that I am going to visit.* One child draws the route on the IP. The other children are encouraged to take part by placing one hand on their tummy if instructions are being drawn correctly and moving their hand to their head if they think the drawing has gone wrong.

3. Repeat as above but without child drawing instructions. *Which animal have I reached?*

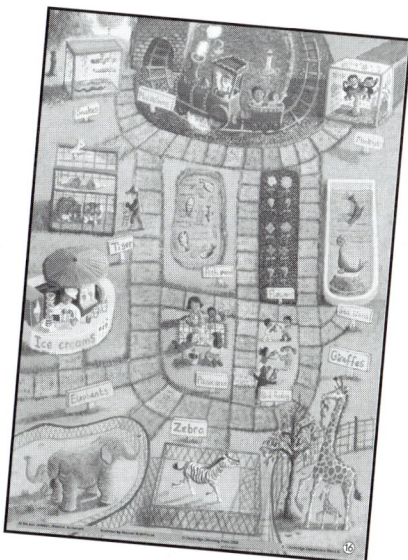

Family activity

- Make a picture of your journey home from school. Put in the things that you go past. Use your picture to tell an adult about your journey.

Related play activity

- Make models of journeys to school using toys or construction kits.

Exploring pattern, shape and space 6.4 Things that turn

Objective ● use everyday words to describe movement

Key idea | Some things turn when they move.

Key words turn, forwards, backwards, right, left

You need
AS 38

collection of objects that turn (e.g. keys, lids and jars, nuts and bolts,
clock with moving hands, cog wheels, wheels on toys and in
construction kits)
floor robot
construction kits
paper, scissors and paper fasteners for Core

Introduction: oral work and mental calculation

Give each child a toy. *I'm going to tell you where to place your toy, so listen carefully. Put your toy beside your ear, … under your leg, … on top of your head, … between your knees, …*

Main teaching input and pupil activities

Direct teaching

1. Show children a collection of objects that turn, e.g. keys, wheel, nuts and bolts, lids on jars, cog wheels, hands on a clock. *How did I make each object move?* (turned it) Discuss how each one is turned. *Can you think of anything else we can turn?* (a door handle, roundabout, ourselves, a page, …) *We are going to look at how things turn and how we can make some things turn. Which things in our collection usually only turn one way?* (hands on the clock) *All the others can turn 2 ways. Can you think why?* Discuss how they tighten and loosen objects, and open and close. *When do the clock hands go the other way?* (If we need to change the time.)

2. Show children the floor robot. *This is a robot, he cannot move on his own but we can tell him what to do and then he will be able to do it.* Show children how the robot can move forwards and backwards. Explain the system for entering the instructions. Invite some children to enter instructions to make the

robot move forwards and backwards. Record them each time so children can refer to them.

3. *Has the robot turned yet?* (No) *We need to give him a different instruction.* Explain and record this for children to refer to. Invite children to enter instructions to make the robot turn. *Where will he will looking (facing) when he has made the turn? I want to make him face Amy: what do I need to tell him to do?*

4. Model how to make the robot move forward, turn and then move forward again. Repeat with children's help. Encourage children to predict which way the robot will face once he has completed the instructions.

Pupil activities

SUPPORT ★ Independent
Give out construction kits with wheels. Ask children to make models with wheels that will turn. They could try to include other parts that can turn.

CORE Adult-supported AS 38
Use AS 38 to make a windmill. Help children to attach it to a straw using a paper fastener. They can then explore ways to make the windmill

turn. *How can you make it turn faster? Will it turn both ways?* Help children to design and make a clock with hands that move (join hands using a paper fastener).

EXTENSION   Adult-led

Develop main teaching with floor robot. Give children opportunities to enter instructions and predict where the robot will face.

How can you tell the robot to … make a square/rectangle? … move to the chair?

Set a course using bricks and ask children to move the robot round it.

Plenary

Key idea: Some things turn when they move.

1. Look at the models made by the support group. Allow children to show how they move by turning the wheels: encourage them to use the word 'turn' when talking about and explaining how their model works. *Will the wheels turn in both directions? Has anyone got another part in their model that can turn?*

2. Ask the extension group to show how they made the floor robot move and turn, explaining what instructions they had to enter. *Did you have any difficulties? What did you do about them?*

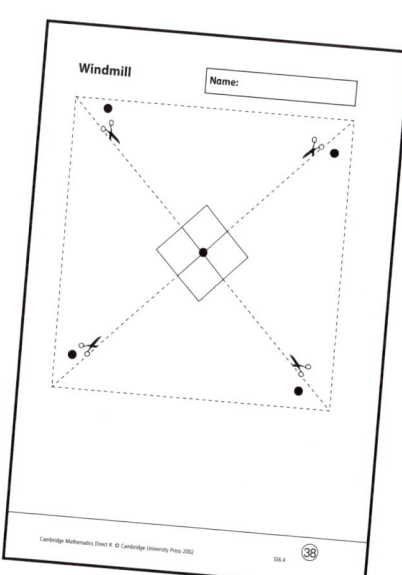

Family activity

● Look at home for things that turn. Draw them.

Related play activity

● Use construction or reclaimed materials to make things that turn.

Exploring pattern, shape and space 6.5 Giving directions

Objectives ● give instructions to other children

Key idea	We can give directions.

Key words   direction, left, right, forwards, sideways, backwards, around, turn

You need   large signs with directions written on for Direct teaching

Introduction: oral work and mental calculation

If working in a large space, ask children to move around the space until you give an instruction, e.g. *Jump 3 times, clap 5 times, step sideways 3 times.* When they have performed the action, they continue to move around.

If space is limited, ask them to perform small actions while sitting, e.g. *Clap 6 times, put your hands under your ears, tap your toes 10 times, put your left hand behind your back, ...*

Main teaching input and pupil activities

Direct teaching

1. Ideally work outside or in hall to allow space for children to move around. *We are going to see how we can give directions to help someone get to a particular place.*

2. *I am going to give you some directions and I want to see if you can follow them.* Give children directions, e.g. *Go forward 4 steps, take 2 steps sideways, turn around and walk forwards 2 steps.*

3. Show children a large piece of paper with instructions (written and drawn), e.g. turn to the door ⌐☐ , forwards 3 steps ↑3 . Ask children to follow the instructions. Repeat.

4. Give children directions with command 'turn' in them. *Which way did you turn? How can we make sure we know which way to turn?* (refer to object or use words left and right) Establish one way for remembering left and right (could be related to hand they use to hold pencil or how index finger and thumb on left hand make letter 'L' when hands are held up as if surrendering). *How far did you*

turn? Agree to stop turning when facing the direction that the left (or right) arm points to when stretched out sideways. Give further instructions using the turn command with left and right.

Ask volunteers to give instructions for moving.

Pupil activities

SUPPORT ★   Adult-supported

Children work in pairs, ideally on the playground or in an open space where they can draw on the ground. If working inside, children will need large sheets of paper to work on. Practise turning right and left (quarter turns as in Direct teaching). Then give simple 3-step directions involving a turn, e.g. forwards 1 steps, turn right, forwards 2 steps. Child A follows the directions and child B draws the trail that child A has made. Child A then returns to the start and child B gives instructions to child A for following the trail. Reverse roles and repeat. Extend to child A giving instructions to child B and then child B giving instructions to child A to follow same trail (establish that 'turn' refers to a quarter turn).

CORE   Adult-led   IP 16

Reinforce knowledge of left and right, e.g. *Show me your right hand, put your left hand on your head, put your right leg in the air, stand on your left leg, wave your right hand, put your right thumb on your nose, ...* Look at IP 16. *What animals can you see?* Place a model person by the tigers. *What if I am standing by the tigers, but I want to go to the monkeys? Who can draw which way to go?* Look at the route. *Who can tell me how to get there?* Take several descriptions: encourage use of left and right. *Has anyone got a different way to draw on the IP?* Take descriptions of the route. Repeat for other starting points and destinations chosen by children. *How many different ways can we find to go from the zebra to the monkey?* Invite children to use a different colour pen to record each different way. Discuss how directions could be given, e.g. referring to objects, counting squares, ... Ask children to work in pairs: give directions to each other for a journey from one part of the classroom to another.

EXTENSION   Independent   AS 39

Ask children to record the route from one animal to another on AS 39 with a line. They should then record instructions. Use differently coloured pencils for each route. Have direction words available for the children to refer to when recording.

Plenary

Key idea: We can give directions.

1. Play 'Simon says' giving directions. This is an opportunity to assess how confident children are in knowing their left and right and which children follow the lead of others rather than making their own decisions. If some children have a problem, ask other children to suggest ways of remembering.

2. Ask children from the extension group to read out the instructions they have written. Children should look at IP 16 and see if they can say which animal they would reach. Praise clear directions. For those instructions that are unclear ask children to help by suggesting another way of giving the instruction. *Which was easier to understand? Why?*

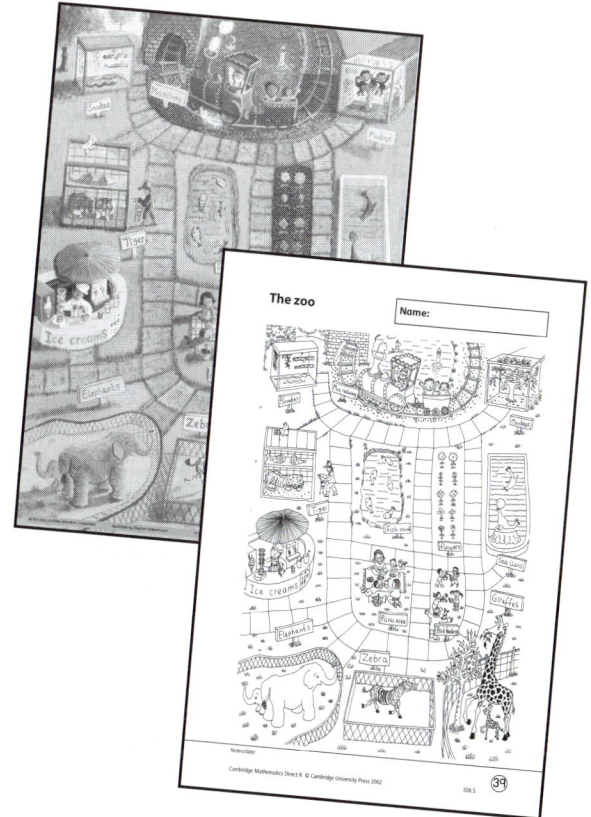

Family activity

- Describe your route as you are travelling, e.g. to school: 'We turn left out of the gate, right at the corner, go along the road, turn right at the shop', ...

Related play activity

- Use the robot, or pretend to be a robot with one child giving instructions for another to follow.